on symbols in anthropology

an anthropological series

edited by jacques maquet

other realities

volume three

undena publications
malibu 1982

on symbols in anthropology
essays in honor
of
harry hoijer
1980

by
james fernandez
melford spiro
milton singer

jacques maquet, editor

published for
the ucla department of anthropology
by
undena publications
malibu 1982

Library of Congress Card Number: 81-52797
ISBN: 0-89003-090-1, paper; 0-89003-091-X, cloth

Undena Publications, P. O. Box 97, Malibu, CA 90265

CONTENTS

THE SYMBOLIC REALM

Jacques Maquet

This volume of essays *On Symbols in Anthropology* has its origin in the second series of The Harry Hoijer Lectures presented by the Department of Anthropology, UCLA, in the Spring of 1980. Professor Spiro's and Professor Fernandez's essays come from the texts of their lectures almost as they were delivered; Professor Singer's essay is a considerably expanded version of his original lecture.

Eleven years before he wrote the article found here, Professor Spiro participated as a discussant in a symposium devoted to "Forms of Symbolic Action." In his comments regarding the papers discussed in that symposium, he expressed disappointment, even frustration, as there had been no attempt in any of them to confront some of the central analytic problems of symbolic anthropology, such as the definition of *symbol*. He also noted that the participants had ignored contributions to symbolic studies made by some of our distinguished predecessors in symbolism, such as Durkheim and Freud, Lloyd Warner and Suzanne Langer [Spiro, 1969:208–9].

The authors of the three essays presented here are not guilty of neglecting definitions and ignoring predecessors. The definitions Singer and Spiro use for *symbol* and other semiotic terms, such as *sign, icon,* and *index,* are derived from Charles Peirce's theory. Fernandez, who neither mentions Peirce here nor in a short and dense article "On the Concept of the Symbol," is also explicit on the meanings of the words he uses [Fernandez, 1975].

The inspiration our authors draw from some of their predecessors is significant. Singer has revealed a specialist's knowledge of Peirce's semiotic in a very recent article [Singer, 1980]. Here, in addition, he extensively analyzes Durkheim's interpretation of totemism and Lloyd Warner's application of totemism to contemporary industrial societies. In fact, Singer's semiotic exploration starts from and pursues Warner's account of Yankee City tercentenary celebration [Warner, 1961]. Spiro and Fernandez choose Freud and Jung respectively as their guides in the understanding of the symbolic realm.

1

Despite different theoretical perspectives, the three contributions collected here may be read as parts of a whole, or almost so. This editor did not expect this convergence as the essays were written independently, without prior consultation or post-lecture discussion. This significant, though imperfect complementarity is based on two factors: the three authors understand the process of *signification* in broadly the same sense, and their papers deal with *different* aspects of the symbolic relation.

The agreement of Singer and Spiro on basic semiotic definitions is complete as each of them uses Peirce's terminology. Like many other social scientists concerned with analyzing phenomena in terms of *signs* and *symbols*, they have adopted the conceptual framework designed last century by Charles Sanders Peirce (1829–1914).

The dominating influence of this famous Harvard logician and mathematician on the social sciences approach to symbolism is less than fortunate. Greenlee, the author of an excellent book on the concept of sign in Peirce's work, expresses the opinion that "much of Peirce's thought on signs is impenetrably obscure" [Greenlee, 1973:5]. A similar conclusion was reached by my graduate students and myself at the end of a three-month seminar devoted to Charles Peirce and Charles Morris as the theoreticians who were at the origin of the American perspective in symbolic anthropology. Drawing one's basic concepts from a deep but obscure thinker belonging to another discipline is fraught with potential difficulties. Certainly Singer and Spiro very skillfully use the Peircian framework; yet I regret that, like Peirce, they ascribe an arbitrary character to the symbol.

Sign, icon, index and *symbol* are the four central terms Singer and Spiro have borrowed from Peirce. In the eight volumes of Peirce's *Collected Papers* there are several definitions of each of these four terms. As this is not the place to enter in lengthy comparisons of the different versions, only one definition per term will be given here.

"A *sign* is anything which is related to a Second thing, its Object, in respect to a Quality, in such a way as to bring a Third thing, its *Interpretant,* into relation to the same Object, and that in such a way as to bring a fourth into relation to that Object in the same form, *ad infinitum*" [Hartshorne & Weiss, 1931–35:vol. 2, par. 92].

In this triadic model *sign* is related to its object as something which refers to something else (about as *sign* is used in the common language). In Saussure's dyadic model, to which Spiro also refers, the relation is between a *signifier* which stands for a *signified*. In fact, *sign* and *signifier* are considered synonymous by our authors; so are *object* and *signified*. *Interpretant,* the third term of the Peircian triad, is less easy to define. According to Greenlee, Peirce "construed 'interpretant' at least as broadly as 'interpretation' is construed in common parlance" [Greenlee, 1973:25]. *Interpretants* are many and Peirce classed them into categories such as energetic, effective, emotional, and ultimate. The following is an example of the ultimate interpretant according to Singer: the final interpretant of an intellectual concept rests in concrete habits [Singer, 1980:490]. As I understand it, the interpretant is the whole semiotic context necessary in order that a particular relation of a sign to its object makes sense. Though the term *interpretation* is an irreducible element of the triadic model, many social scientists who use the Peircian terminology seem to ignore it.

An *icon* is a sign which "stands for something merely because it resembles it" [Hartshorne & Weiss, 1931–35:vol. 3, par. 362]. The relation of similarity between an icon and its object may be a resemblance in visual appearance; in this case the icon is an *image*. It may also be a similarity of internal organization between the elements of the iconic sign and its object, as in *maps* and *diagrams*.

An *index* is "a sign which refers to the Object that it denotes by virtue of being really affected by that Object" [ibid., vol. 2, par. 248]. The height of a mercury column in a thermometer is an *index* of temperature; symptoms of a disease are *indices* of that disease. Spiro interprets the indexical relation as "factual contiguity."

A *symbol* is "a sign which refers to the Object that it denotes by virtue of a law, usually an association of general ideas, which operates to cause the Symbol to be interpreted as referring to that Object" [ibid., vol. 2, par. 249]. Singer and Spiro understand, as other social scientists do, that "by virtue of a law" is meant "by a conventional code." The stars and stripes flag stands for the United States of America by agreement among American citizens represented by their Congress. Words in the vocabulary of a language are symbols which refer to what they signify by agreement among the speakers of that language. A conventional code has to be learned since the connection between the flag and the country is arbitrary; so is the connection between a word and what it denotes (except in the few cases of onomatopœic formation).

Defining *symbol* as an arbitrary sign is characteristic of the logical approach to semiotics. In the tradition of the humanities there is, on the contrary, a natural relationship between the symbolic signifier and what it signifies, as Lalande described it in the collective dictionary by the *Société française de Philosophie* [1947:1058]. In the same work, Brunschvicg wrote that "symbol is opposed to artificial sign in that it possesses an internal power of representation; for example the serpent biting its tail as symbol of eternity" [ibid., trans. by J.M.].

Though he does not directly address the question of the arbitrary or natural character of the symbol, Fernandez's conception of it belongs to what I call here the humanistic tradition. Fernandez prefers the term *sign-image* to *symbol* and throughout his essay deals with what Peirce would have called *icons*. And icons, though they may be polysemic, do not have arbitrary meanings. In our everyday language *darkness at the bottom of the stairs* may have different significations, such as mystery, protected place, or access to an underworld; but none of them is arbitrary and none requires learning a conventional code.

Despite definitions derived from two traditions, the one of logic and the one of the humanities, our three contributors agree on the basic notion of *sign* as something which stands for something else. Beyond that, terminology separates Spiro and Singer from Fernandez. Suppose a painting of Mount Fuji is perceived by the beholders as expressing the ideas of majesty and steadfastness (that is, as a sign standing for these ideas); it will be referred to as *symbol* in the humanistic tradition and the ordinary language, as *icon* in the Peircian perspective, and as *sign-image* (or simply as *image*) by Fernandez. The same painting seen as a depiction of Mount Fuji (that is, as a sign standing for Mount Fuji) will be referred to as *image* along the logical and humanistic lines; I do not know what word Fernandez would use, as *image* has for him the connotation just mentioned.

A lack of common terminology does not prevent our authors from focusing their attention on phenomena "located" in a common field, the *symbolic realm*. These phenomena are emblematic artifacts and cultural performances for Singer, collective and mental representations for Spiro, and inner imagery for Fernandez.

2

The order in which the three essays appear in this volume makes it possible to read them as parts of a whole.

Fernandez's paper comes first because it clearly sets the distinction between two fundamental modes of thinking, the analogic and the discursive. This dichotomy is to be recognized at the onset of any study of symbolism, as it puts it in proper perspective. Symbols are often discussed as if they were only figures of speech which allow understanding by indirection. Symbols are that, but more importantly, they are supports of a mode of thinking which proceeds according to a logic different from the one used in rational discourse. Fernandez likes to contrast these two modes as *visual* and *verbal*. Other frequently used terms, besides *analogic* and *discursive,* are *metaphoric* and *rational,* or *by images* and *by concepts*.

Another reason to read Fernandez first is that he expresses some of the main themes of the humanistic tradition (which is reflected by the common language). One theme is that the symbolic process gives access to the invisible and the intangible. Majesty and steadfastness cannot be seen or touched but Mount Fuji, or a painting of it, can suggest what these moral qualities mean. Symbols are material things which stand for nonmaterial objects. For Fernandez, symbolism is a way, even the only way, to the inchoate "at once undefinable and impulsive." Although this is not the place to discuss the term *inchoate,* so central to Fernandez's thinking, the first strategy for approaching the inchoate is to consider the images upon which it is predicated. It should be mentioned here, however, that Fernandez emphasizes the importance of a traditionally recognized function of symbols: they mediate between what is perceived by the senses and what is built in the mind.

Another basic theme highlighted by Fernandez is the multivocality (or polysemy) of symbolic signs: one symbol stands for more than one object (or class of objects). Darkness symbolizes depth and chaos, death and evil, austerity and formality, and some other ideas. There is no one-to-one relationship between symbolic signifiers and their objects. Fernandez's view of ambiguity, uncertainty, and shiftiness as rooted in the nature of the mind, suggests an ontologic foundation to the polysemic character of symbols. These metaphysical views do not have to be adopted to recognize the polysemy of symbols, but they certainly "dramatize" it.

Scholars write on symbolism in a discursive, not in a figurative mode. Fernandez makes use of both modes: in a discursive framework, he inserts figurative sequences. This approach gives the reader a welcome taste of symbolic style. Fernandez is, as he says, a "visualizer," and his paper proceeds from one thematic imagery to another: from the dark at the top of the stairs to Jung's house, to the Fang ladder, and to the stables in the mountain villages of northern Spain. He demonstrates how images can be organized in an argument and can solve a problem by moving from one context to another.

3

With Spiro's essay, we take a closer look at the type of existence—"in" or "outside" the mind—of the nonmaterial signified. He does not address this question as such, but what he discusses here—an explanation of the religious actors' belief in the external existence of the mythico-religious world of their tradition—is an excellent approach to this central problem of symbolism.

Spiro already stated in a previous article that "the differentiating characteristic of religion is the belief in superhuman beings" [1966:95]. It conforms to his views, I think, to add that these superhumans, as they do not belong to the everyday sensory experience of the believers, are denoted by verbal and visual signs. Such are names *(Krishna, Jesus, the Buddha,* or *God),* human forms (a handsome flute player, a tortured victim nailed on a cross, a meditator sitting in a cross-legged position, or an impressive elderly man with a white beard), or emblems (a trident for Shiva, the Greek letter *ikhthus* for Christ, an empty throne for the Buddha, or a triangle for the Trinity).

These signs are sensible (audible or visible) and they stand for nonmaterial objects. In symbolism, the signified objects are mental contents or collective representations. For instance, *Krishna* stands for devotional self-surrender, *Jesus* for the ultimate sacrifice of love, *the Buddha* is the archetype of man perfected by enlightenment, and *God* stands for the idea of the unconditioned. Now, for the religious believers, the signified objects are entities having an external existence: in some other realm these superhuman beings exist on their own, independently from the ideas we have of them in our minds. In that case, the sensible signs (names, pictures, statutes, and emblems) are not symbols but *referents* which designate actual and concrete, though nonmaterial beings. Just as my name refers to me but does not symbolize me.

The conception of religion as belief in the existence of superhuman beings used by Spiro, is an excellent operational definition. As an indicator, it may be easily applied by several observers. Furthermore, it clarifies our understanding of the phenomenon of signification. Signs standing for nonmaterial objects have a different conceptual status if these objects are construed as mental ("in the mind"), or are believed to exist concretely outside the mind. It is appropriate, I surmise, to call the former *symbols* and the latter, *referents.*

This distinction is useful also to clearly differentiate two ways to adhere to a tradition of thought and practice, the *religious* and the *spiritual,* and consequently two classes among those who identify themselves with such a tradition: those who take the great figures to be actual entities, and those who take them to be symbolic ones. (Incidentally this is a question different from whether in the past the great figures were historical, as Jesus or Siddhartha Gautama, or not, as Shiva or Krishna; in either case, at present they are actual or symbolic figures.) For most of the villagers of Sri Lanka, the Buddha statues refer to a living presence; whereas for spiritually advanced monks and lay persons, the statues stand for the enlightened state they hope to attain.

In some traditions, Hinduism or Buddhism for instance, the religious and spiritual attitudes are considered legitimate. In others, the Judaic-Christian-Islamic world for instance, the symbolic interpretation has usually been condemned by the authorities as heretical.

Spiro's essay contributes to the study of symbolism by making us aware of the two kinds of existence that may be attributed to the nonmaterial signifieds. A distinction of consequence as it led some followers to be burnt at the stake and others to be beheaded.

4

Singer's essay on emblems of identity explores another essential aspect of symbolism—how the relation between a symbol and its object affects those who state it and those who perceive it. He is particularly interested in finding out how emblematic signs, such as "Yankees" and "ethnics," "oldtimers" and "newcomers," are used to delimit social groups in a New England town.

In many studies on symbolism little attention is paid to the human subjects associated to a symbolic system: those who establish the relationship of symbolic signification between a sign and its object, and those who see the symbols and understand what they stand for.

In Saussure's dyadic relationship between signifier and signified, the subjects establishing the relationship and those "reading" it are not given much heed. Peirce's triadic model of sign, object, and interpretant does not include human subjects either. Singer, who has adopted this triadic construct, gives more emphasis to the Peircian *utterers* and *interpreters* than Peirce himself. In a recent article, Singer states that "everything that is present to our minds should appear as a sign of ourselves as well as a sign of something without us" [Singer, 1980:490]. Singer's pentadic model is a timely reminder that symbolism is also communication. Messages are sent by utterers (the painter of the picture of Mount Fuji) and received by interpreters (the beholders who interpret the Mount Fuji painting as a symbol of majesty and steadfastness).

Singer's inclusion of the subjects in his model is a contribution to symbolism. Indeed the connection between symbol and object exists *only* in the minds of those who belong to a social group. A community of minds is the condition of *any* signification, and not only of the signification requiring the knowledge of a conventional code. There has been some confusion between the social *consensus* and the learning of a particular *code*. When humanistic scholars speak of a *natural* relationship between a signifier and its signified (as opposed to an *arbitrary* one), they do not claim that this connaturalness is to be perceived outside of any cultural context. Any person who has shared for some time the culture of Sri Lanka will perceive flags and other festive trimmings of a yellowy orange color as related to a monastic celebration, simply because of the natural similarity in color of the flags and the monks' robes. Connaturalness is perceived outside any code but within a specific cultural context.

It is not irrespective of his or her culture that a man or a woman will interpret symbols. When some symbols are "read" the same way by interpreters from different cultures (the Mount Fuji painting is a symbol of majesty and steadfastness for people from many cultures other than the Japanese), it is not because the signification is rooted in a metacultural human nature, but because the same kind of signifier (a towering and broad-based mountain) belongs to the collective experience of many societies.

Singer's focus on the communities creating and understanding symbols helps us realize that the cultural consensus of a group should be clearly distinguished from an arbitrary conventional code. Utterers and interpreters are always cultural actors even when they are involved in transcultural symbolism.

When considering the three essays in this book as clarifications of different aspects of symbolism, Singer's article appears as a contribution focused on the human component in symbolic transactions. For social classes and other subdivisions of a society, symbols have a powerful function of identification. By means of cultural performances and emblems, each segment of a contemporary city tells to itself and the other segments who their members are and from whom they are separated.

*   *   *

In this introduction, I have attempted to emphasize the continuity of the three essays, to present them as parts of a joint enterprise in spite of terminological differences, and to indicate how they converge on a common ground, the symbolic realm.

The essays were not meant to completely cover that realm, but in fact they survey a good part of it. What is achieved does not have the consistency and smooth flow of a one-author book, but instead has the liveliness and genuineness of primary sources. Together, they constitute an advanced introduction to symbolic anthropology for those who have already trodden the field and would like to compare their views with some conclusions of three eminent scholars.

ACKNOWLEDGEMENT

In my task of editor of this volume, I have been immeasurably helped by Nancy Cutler Daniels's patient, meticulous, and cheerful assistance.

REFERENCES

Fernandez, James W.
   1975   On the Concept of the Symbol. *Current Anthropology* (Chicago), 16(4):652–654.

Greenlee, Douglas
   1973   *Peirce's Concept of the Sign.* The Hague: Mouton.

Hartshorne, Charles and Paul Weiss, eds.
   1931– *Collected Papers of Charles Sanders Peirce.* Vols. 1–6.
   1935   Cambridge, Mass.: Harvard University Press.

Lalande, André, ed.
   1947   *Vocabulaire technique et critique de la philosophie.* 5th ed., Paris: Presses Universitaires de France (for the Société française de Philosophie).

Singer, Milton
   1980   Signs of the Self: An Exploration in Semiotic Anthropology. *American Anthropologist* (Washington, D.C.), 82(3):485–507.

Spiro, Melford E.
   1966   Religion: Problems of Definition and Explanation. In *Anthropological Approaches to the Study of Religion,* ed. by Michael Banton. London: Tavistock Publications (A.S.A. Monographs), pp. 85–126.

   1969   Discussion. In *Forms of Symbolic Action,* ed. by Robert F. Spencer. Seattle: University of Washington Press (for the American Ethnological Society), pp. 208–214.

Warner, W. Lloyd
   1961   *The Family of God: A Symbolic Study of Christian Life in America.* New Haven: Yale University Press.

THE DARK AT THE BOTTOM OF THE STAIRS: THE INCHOATE IN SYMBOLIC INQUIRY AND SOME STRATEGIES FOR COPING WITH IT

James W. Fernandez

Wish I was a Kellogg's Cornflake
Floatin' in my bowl takin' movies,
Relaxin' awhile, livin' in style,
Talkin' to a raisin who 'casionn'ly
    plays L.A.,
Casually glancing at his toupee.
Wish I was an English muffin
'Bout to make the most out of a toaster.
I'd ease myself down,
Comin' up brown.
I prefer boysenberry
More than any ordinary jam.
I'm a "Citizens for Boysenberry Jam" fan.
Ah, South California.
If I become a first lieutenant
Would you put my photo on your piano?
To Maryjane—
Best wishes, Martin.
(Old Roger draft-dodger
Leavin' by the basement door),
Everybody knows what he's
Tippy-toeing down there for.

Simon & Garfunkel,
"Punky's Dilemma"

"But underground nothing ran straight.
All the tunnels curved, split, rejoined,
branched, interlaced, looped, traced
elaborate routes that ended where they
began for there was no beginning and
no end, for there was nowhere to get
to. There was no center, no heart to
the maze."

Ursula Kroeber LeGuin,
The Tombs of Atuan

I hope the reader will forgive me the abundance of epigraphs[1]—
perhaps a surfeit—that accompany my argument but they are necessary
because, as Freud would tell us, our subject, the inchoate in human
experience, is "over-determined." I have been arguing for some years,
in respect to symbolic analyses, that the inchoate is categorical and
irreducible in human affairs—an uncharted and imperfectly charitable
hinterland to thought and feeling which nevertheless exerts its pleni-
potentiary attractions and repulsions upon us, impelling us to those
recurrent but ultimately unsatisfying predications of objects upon subjects, and vice versa—which is so characteristic of our humanity. But
the subject matter of our existence in all its numinosity is, in actual
fact, inchoate, neither black nor white but gray matter, as it is said.

Naturally I have been under some pressure about this notion of the
inchoate, however privileged and irreducible I have tried to make it.
Critics of my position have taken the centrality of this term as an
instance of my incomprehensibility or obscurantism. But the fault is
not mine. As far as symbolic processes are concerned, it is in the
nature of the mind itself. Still and perhaps, something more might be
said about the inchoate than I have managed to say. So I will try here
to say something more without pretending to say anything final or
definitive.

[1] The one, "Punky's Dilemma," being in my view one of the "deepest songs"
of the Vietnam War generation; the other is very apt for our argument here and is also
suggestive of where the anthropological patrimony might lead.

I should also say something about my method of composition here. Of course, I want to say something more about the inchoate so I must organize my materials to that end. But I also wish to be true to my subject matter and get at what it actually means to me. It means first of all a set of images—and I ought to confess here that I tend to be at incipient moments of thought a visualizer rather than a verbalizer. The inchoate is for me first of all the dark at the bottom of the stairs, and subsequently to it being that, whatever that is, it is all the other images and contexts that are swung into association with that central and organizing image to cast light upon it—and which are part of its polysemy and overdetermined quality. The epigraphs that appear here suggest some of these contexts.

I would go on to argue moreover that this method of argument—an argument of images really—is typical of symbolic problem-solving generally that verbalizers, of which our academies are full, of course, tend to overlook. One has a problem of action or explanation in life. One doesn't always have to put a label upon it as, for example, the problem of the inchoate. An image is generated by pictorializing the problem. This image can be satisfying in and of itself. For a picture solves a problem for an essentially visual animal like Homo Sapiens to whom "seeing is believing." Or a picture can lead out by association to other contexts and other pictures. Or an image can be acted out. We do it all the time. In any event, this paper begins in images which have led to other images. As explanation and argument it is an acting out of images. When you created a problem for me by asking me, a middlewesterner more or less, rooted on the East Coast, to fly clear across the country to South California to talk to you about symbolism, I responded pretty much as most of my informants in various revitalization movements responded when I plagued them with problems of symbolic understanding.

"All we see is the living room where
the action takes place. There is a
flight of stairs at the far left . . .
at the top the upstairs hallway.
During the daytime scenes this small
area is in semi-darkness and at night
it is black . . . we are conscious of this
area throughout the play as though it
holds some possible threat to the characters."

William Inge,
The Dark at the Top of the Stairs.

"The two skulls my dear friend Carl
Gustaf, what do you make of them?"

Freud to Jung

I hope the reader will permit a glancing reference to my cultural
roots here—Henry County, Spoon River, western Illinois—for the
images we generate to solve problems are always, in part, a function
of our primordial experiences and the cultural ecology of our upbring-
ing. Because of its resonance with that locale and the family romances
characteristic of it, William Inge's play of the late 1950s, *The Dark
at the Top of the Stairs,* was very powerful for me. It must have been
mainly in my mind here. The house and the small Oklahoma town
described in this play are very familiar. I know about the dark at the
top of the stairs.

But what I know is rather different from what William Inge knows
or at least what his various characters know. The dark has a significantly
different meaning for each character according to their sex and age
(I hope the reader will forgive me for passing over a central and
powerful statement in the play about small town anti-semitism and
color consciousness). For Reenie, the painfully shy 16-year-old just
coming out of her chrysalis, the dark is the sheltering comfort of her
microcosm, her own bed and bedroom removed from the glare of the

drawing room downstairs and motherly pressures toward social engage-
ment as well as male stares and male assessments of her developing
charms. For the 12-year-old Sonny, his mother's favorite, already drawing room wise, the dark is that "some'then awful," an imagined mons-
ter of his infant years projected into the uncertainties of the future—
once and future dreads. For the parents, Cora and her rough-mannered
traveling salesman husband, Ruben, the dark—and this is surely sensed
by their children—is their connubial situation, the pleasures and the
domestic politics, the dominations and the subordinations of lovemak-
ing in a marriage "by sex redeemed." In the final scene Rubin, cel-
ebrating his homecoming, calls to his wife from the top of the stairs.
Only his bare feet can be seen by the light from the drawing room
lamps. If Levi-Strauss was in the audience I suppose he would lean
forward to see if one of those feet was slightly clubbed.

I take time to detail this scenario not only because, as I was warned,
I had picked a bad title for Californians who, living in ranch houses,
are going to have little experience of stairs—but because I want to
make clear that we are, as is characteristic of symbols, in the presence
of polysemy. Within this play the dark condenses within itself past and
future, comfort and threat, connubiality and virginity, loneliness and
intensification, self-realization and the subordination of the sexual
bond.

The more familiar symbol is the dark at the bottom of the stairs.
Successful writers employ it with frequency. It appears appropriately
enough in Agatha Christie's last and posthumous novel, *Sleeping Murder* (1976) as it does in Ursula Kroeber LeGuin's *The Tombs of Atuan*
(1975), an anthropological science fiction in which the characters struggle against a sterile devotion to the dark labyrinth and black undertomb
of an ancient religion. In these books the dark at the bottom of the
stairs is both symbol and the actual scene of action showing us that
subtle connection always present in symbolic analysis between the
representative and the performative—between the syntagmatic of the
scenario and the paradigmatics of our understanding—between models
of and models for.

For the student of human nature, the most compelling instance of
that dark to which we are turned is Jung's famous dream which he

recounted to Freud on the seven-week 1909 voyage to America for the
Clark University visit. During that period, in the spirit of master and
disciple, they were recounting each other's dreams for the benefit of
mutual analysis. Already Jung was noting a defensiveness in the master
in free associating to his (Freud's) own dreams—an unwillingness to
risk his authority and a tendency to place that authority above the truth.
At the same time Freud in Jung's view seemed to be inordinately drawn
to certain elements in Jung's dreams that had to do with death wishes
possibly held towards the master himself. Here is an abbreviated form
of the dream which we might otherwise remark was of central importance to Jung in developing his later ideas of the "collective unconscious."

> This was the dream. I was in a house I did not know, which
> had two stories. It was "my house." I found myself in the
> upper story, where there was a kind of salon furnished with
> fine old pieces in rococo style. On the walls hung a number
> of precious old paintings. I wondered that this should be my
> house, and thought, "Not bad." But then it occurred to me
> that I did not know what the lower floor looked like.
> Descending the stairs, I reached the ground floor. There
> everything was much older, and I realized that this part of
> the house must date from about the fifteenth or sixteenth
> century. The furnishing were medieval; the floors were of
> red brick. Everywhere it was rather dark. I went from one
> room to another, thinking, "Now I really must explore the
> whole house." I came upon a heavy door, and opened it.
> Beyond it, I discovered a stone stairway that led down into
> the cellar. Descending again, I found myself in a beautifully
> vaulted room which looked exceedingly ancient. Examining
> the walls, I discovered layers of brick among the ordinary
> stone blocks, and chips of brick in the mortar. As soon as
> I saw this I knew that the walls dated from Roman times.
> My interest by now was intense. I looked more closely at
> the floor. It was of stone slabs, and in one of these I dis-
> covered a ring. When I pulled it, the stone slab lifted, and
> again I saw a stairway of narrow stone steps leading down
> into the depths. These, too, I descended, and entered a low

cave cut into the rock. Thick dust lay on the floor, and in the dust were scattered bones and broken pottery, like remains of a primitive culture. I discovered two human skulls, obviously very old and half disintegrated. Then I awoke. [Jung 1963:182–3.]

Freud's response to this elaborated dream was to query Jung repeatedly about the two skulls. "What did I think about them. And whose were they?" For Jung, the dream led primarily into deeper and deeper levels of the paleo-unconscious rather than out to the residue of contemporary relationships. It led to the world of primitive man within him. "I saw from this that (Freud) was completely helpless in dealing with certain kinds of dreams and had to take refuge in his doctrine (and his fantasies of father murder). It was up to me to find the *real* meaning of the dream." So Jung lied to Freud to put him at ease—or so he thought.

What was the *real* meaning of the dream? Freudians and Jungians have been locked in primal struggle ever since. The point is that the dream has at the least several meanings. And the "real" meaning is that interpretation which is apt and useful—manageable—for a given situation. For Freud, subjected as he was to the uncertainties of his relation to his assertive younger colleague, the motivated interpretation had to do with death wishes and parricide. That was most useful in helping him to deal with an uncertain and pressing personal situation. For Jung, whose mind was steeped in his own historical and prehistorical training, an interpretation that organized that superabundant content was most strategic—and only mildly parricidal in its reshaping of Freud's view of the unconscious. (After all, Jung was only a "little bit pregnant" with his system at the time.)

In the interpretation of complex symbolic matters we are always in the presence of the motivating principle of strategic or pragmatic understanding. Symbols are generated out of a need, whether a life wish or a death wish, but there is no real interpretation that is not situational and strategic. To suppose that there is a real or true interpretation that surpasses situation and the primal preoccupations of a given participant is the first strategy by which the inchoate has been

approached. We may call it the adversarial strategy or the zero-sum
strategy which presumes that there will be winners and losers in symbolic analysis—the rights and the wrongs, the reals and the illusorys.
Such strategists by eloquence or sheer brass may enjoy temporary
parricidal or fratricidal victories but in the long run the scenario shifts
and circumstances alter cases. In symbolic analysis the abhorrence of
the excluded middle which we inherit from Aristotelian logic is mis-
placed. Things are both/and, and everything in the epistemological
sense is illusory. The real illusion, we have to put it that way, is the
one that is apt and edifying for its epoch or situation. Judgement in
symbolic analysis is much less empirical than moral.

2

"The Prince of Paris has
Lost His Hat and Some Say
This and Some Say That and
I Say Number Five, Number
Five to the Foot!
Who Sir Me Sir?
Yes Sir You Sir!
No Sir Not I Sir!
Then Who Sir?
Number 1 Sir
Ahh, Number 1 to the Foot."

(Middlewestern children's game)

There's a bit of a trick, isn't there, in what we have just put forth?
For while we have cut ourselves off from any Archimedean point
that would give us uncontestable epistemological purchase on the symbolic world, we still hold onto the possibility of edifying, and perhaps
privileged, interpretation of the symbolic—for a certain time and place,
of course. Indeed, we *have to* privilege that interpretation because we
need it amidst the invevitable shiftiness of human social life. Role
theory has long taught us that even within the confines of the domestic

unit—and even within happy families, let alone unhappy ones and ones as in present day America, undergoing challenging changes in sex roles—there is role ambiguity and role conflict as between being a mother and/or a wife, a son and/or a brother. Primal scenes are the working out of these ambiguities amidst the added urgency of biological impulse. It is just these kinds of shifts of family role and social status as between daughtership and prospective mate, motherhood and connubial partnership that our play *The Dark at the Top of the Stairs* most intentfully explores. The yearly cycle and the life cycle rites of passage and of intensification show us the celebration of the ambiguities of identity and the shapeshiftings from status to status. And of course when the institutional structures of civilization preempt the primacy of the family we have the added Antigonian ambiguities and discontents as between filial and civic responsibility; as between nurturant fatherhood or attentive husbandhood and a respected and authoritative professional life; and as between being a homebody and a helpmeet or a pert business associate. Life is inchoate in that sense and requires of us all that we be shapeshifters. And it is out of that incessant requirement, as well as to it, that a great deal of symbolic material is generated and addressed; presenting to our imaginations our condition in some graspable form so that we might somehow better deal with it, understand our moral responsibilities in the face of it.

This shapeshifting or shiftiness (see Fernandez 1975:652–4)—just to be mischievous—in the human equation not only rests in our multiple and often conflicting roles, domestic and civic, nor only upon the ephemeralness of our physiological states in life cycles and natural cycles; but it also rests upon the cardinal role of duplicity, as Jakobson (n.d.) calls it, in language and the use of language—the incessant interplay of message and code, narrated event and speech event. There is a particular class of grammatical units of which the personal pronouns are examples, *par excellence,* in which message and code are particularly intertwined. Jakobson called these "shifters." As the word "I" shifts from speaker to speaker, its referent shifts completely for it is part of the message that is not only conventional but is tied in with the speech event, the code itself. The "I" like any personal pronoun is in subjective and existential relation with the speech event at the same time that it is an objective and conventional part of the message. Shifters thus are a part of the linguistic code which make a particular comment upon the message in which they are contained and are particularly forceful examples of the duplicity of which Jakobson speaks. The duplicity and shiftiness contained in the personal pronouns—their subjective-objective or indexical-symbolic quality—is what makes them difficult for children to learn. Something of the uncertainty, even anxiety, they provoke is contained in this rapid fire and accusatory children's game, with its quick interplay of subjective and objective pronouns and under pressure its quick and quite human transference of blame, which we have used as an epigraph in this section of our argument.

In the shapeshifting required of us in ongoing social life and in the duplicity of our language, there reposes then this recurrent dilemma, impending disorder, moral uncertainty—the inchoate in its social and linguistic form. Now a common strategy for dealing with this phrasing of the inchoate is to presume that these productions conceal a set of normative principles or rules for behavior which the participant can detect and which will act to defeat ambiguity and steer him through the seas of social uncertainty to social trustworthiness and predictability. We can call it the didactive strategy which studies symbolic action for the rules contained in it. Of course some symbolic productions are plainly didactive hortatory, ethically normative in this way. But a commandment-oriented people like we Judeo-Christians, and also a people so committed to wiring diagrams, rulebooks, and flowcharts as we are, should be cautious here. Most symbolic productions are not only normative or are not really normative in this way. Surely not the most interesting ones. Most symbolic productions act more to excite the moral imagination than to alert it to its duty—arousing participants to a contemplation and greater tolerance of the centrality of ambiguity, paradox, and dilemma in the human condition. As much auguries of ambiguity as templates of conduct, they "edify, we might say, by puzzlement," stimulating us to trustworthy solidarities by showing us the potential disorder in our social and intellectual natures —reconfirming us in our commitment to accustomed material gratifications. Of course, the situation is volatile and our moral imagination can be so stimulated as to seek for new, and often revolutionary, solidarities heretofore unrealized.

Surely this is the lesson in the widespread trickster figure—the shapeshifter *par excellence*—whose extravagant and irrepressible actions are hardly models for any acceptable everyday behaviour; but whose outrageous qualities excite our imaginations to the apprehension of something existential in the human condition—something that continually confronts us and is in us and lies behind and below the niceties of a well-structured social life. The trickster is the "type" symbolic figure, fleshing out the contrarieties which lie in the inchoate. He is exceptional in delineation, to be sure. Still, he or she is simply the more striking instance of the complex possibilities that symbolic statements so often ask us to imagine.

Recently in the literature, a number of us have been raising the question of anthropology's relation to the moral imagination. On the one hand we have wondered whether those who, like Victor Turner, perform dramatistic analyses of human behavior do not in laying out social dramas, invest that behavior with a moral structure that in all actuality—the humdrum mini-max situations of everyday life—it does not possess (see Fernandez 1975a). This moralistic impulse comes particularly to the fore in Turner's recent work on martyrdom and pilgrimage, where social dramas turn into the "via crucis" and where we find the subjects of inquiry taking up the martyr's role—submitting themselves to a preordained scenario of dramatic denouement. One wonders whether these dramas are more in the author and his own moral imagination, already richly stimulated by a lifetime of saints' legends, than in the materials themselves. Important as it may be for the survival of culture that the recounters of legends, the tellers of tales, and the crafters of plays provide such dramatic antidotes to our inveterate self-interest, one asks whether the exercises of such moral imagination in self and its excitement in others is the particular challenge of anthropological science.

There are those who answer, resoundingly, Yes! And indeed one must agree with Clifford Geertz (1977) that anthropology has a particular power to exercise the moral imagination as we, by arresting narratives of other's lifeways, bring pressure to bear upon our own, showing alternate ways of working out human dilemmas and creating a renewed sense of the potentialities of our humanity. Particularly in the highly civilized societies—and I use the term only to refer to those societies with a high degree of overt and compulsive emphasis on organization and order and with correspondingly powerful tendencies toward one dimensionality and the lowest common denominator—are anthropological accounts a necessary antidote, though perhaps only a palliative, to the constriction of the human spirit. If there are some anthropologists who feel in our calling the impulse to moving narration and the dramatic craft, there is sufficient narrow-minded and self-interested temporizing mediocrity in modern life to justify such exercises of the moral imagination.

But the point, really, is that whatever set and scenario we construct on the main floor of our experience, there remain at the bottom of the stairs such dilemmas and ambiguities of social and personal life, such shapeshifting, as to offer no permanent resolution good for all seasons. Symbolic productions speak to that inchoate condition, at once providing us with images which we can perform so as to act our way through those intense moments in life (the sacred ones—in which dilemmas, ambiguities, and problems ultimately unresolvable threaten to overwhelm us); while at the same time they expand our awareness and temper our intolerance for such incongruities and incompatibilities. We are of course in this Western World, creators of a masterful culture which would put such disorder as is suggested here out upon the peripheries of life or seek to extirpate it whenever we find it rising up out of the basement. But I think that Tom Beidleman is just right, in a recent discussion relating the trickster to the moral imagination, in insisting upon the centrality of ambiguity and uncertainty (see Beidleman 1980). It is our tendency to see the trickster as a fraud, a social cheat, an outcast. The more often, and perhaps in the more perceptive cultures, he stands not in some far off closet but at the very center—dancing and pranking, wisecracking at the very top of the stairs.

3

"A society is similar to a
house, divided into rooms
and corridors. The more a
society resembles our own
form of civilization the
thinner are its partitions
and the more open are its
doors of communication."

Van Gennep,
The Rites of Passage

The moral imagination is one thing; the scientific imagination is
quite another. Of course, the two can be confused. Science can be a
sacred cow. But it is one thing to be confronted with our existential
condition in all its complexity, paradox, and ambiguity. It is another
thing to seek models as simple and clear and as isomorphic with the
reality as possible. The moral imagination is full of rhetorical intent
and seeks to excite persons and groups. The scientific imagination
seeks to represent reality in such a way as to better manipulate things
as well as to predict the course of their development. The probing and
disclosing of essential structures in as parsimonious a way as possible
is the main objective of the scientific imagination. One might go on
to say that the moral imagination mainly promotes our humility while
the scientific imagination excites our sense of power, were it not that
we find so many humble scientists and arrogant moralists.

As an instance of the scientific imagination probing the structure
of realities, I remember a conversation with the late Hadley Cantril,
an eminent social psychologist and, I might add, personally anything
but arrogant. Professor Cantril was proposing to take his self-anchoring
scale to Africa. He asked me, ingenuously, about the Africans'
acquaintance with ladders as well as about their orientation toward
them. As will be remembered, the self-anchoring scale seeks to get
at attitudes towards past, present, and future by having informants find
themselves on a ladder. Where are you now? Where were you? Where

will you be? The bottom of the ladder is taken as the worst conceivable way of life and the top the best.

I could only be helpful by pointing out that in two closely related branches of the same Fang religious movement in Africa there was dark, as it were, both at the bottom and at the top of the ladder. The New Life branch dug a grave pit behind the altar down into whose obscurity the membership descended in order to commune with the ancestors and obtain the word. The dark at the bottom of the ladder! In another branch, Dissoumba, a small dark chamber was constructed at the apex of the roof. The sacred Ngombi chestharp was kept in that chamber gathering the power of the ancestors and the great gods who hovered at the apex of the chapel. A ladder was put up to it before the all-night rituals and the harp was passed down to the harpist on the floor of the chapel. The dark at the top of the ladder.

It would be pretty hard to anticipate, I counseled, where a given African culture would locate the dark end of the ladder. It would be a harder thing yet to determine just what was meant by the dark and how it could be related to the good life and to past, present, and future. "From darkness we come and to darkness we will return" seemed to me a fair summary of much Bwiti belief.

My answer to Cantril was essentially what we have come to know as a structuralist answer: The concreteness of existential meaning is subordinated to underlying structures for it is not the concrete referent of our terms that is interesting—it is the relationship between them. It is not so important what the ends of the ladder mean; it is the fact that the ends of the ladder and the ladder itself constitute a system of understanding—ladders are good to think with and stairs, too, I suppose. There can hardly be a better structuralist symbol, in fact. The ladder has polarity, a satisfying binary quality. It has mediation. And best of all it has what structuralist studies rarely have—measurement along an equally divided continuum.

The structuralist strategy in symbolic inquiry, we can be brief about it, has the effect of draining symbols of much of their content—vitiating the plenitude of their resonances, the suggestive tension of their over-determination. It is a strategy that makes, for example, out of all the superabundance of associations contained in the trickster figure a mere mediator, an operator rather than a human existence personified. In some respects the structuralist strategy in the face of the symbolic is familiar to us. It is the logico-deductive strategy of Western man and modern science even though, in other respects as we see below, it does not follow through to state clearly the causes and conditions of its object of inquiry. It is a strategy, Levi-Strauss tells us in *Tristes Tropiques* (1955), that by an "effort of understanding destroys the object of its attention." This phrase can have several meanings, but because of the penchant in structuralism to reduce existential complexities to their essence it may be justly accused of an "evasion of realities," of alienation and inauthenticity.[2] On the other hand it has been frequently criticised for its free and easy way with ethnographic data and for creative misinterpretation in laying out structures of opposition and transformation (see Thomas, Kronenfeld and Kronenfeld 1976).

This is hardly the place to give the structuralist strategy its due. It *is* worth reiterating that a method so essential vitiates the rich and overdetermined surface texture of symbolic activity and always risks beguiling its practitioners into a false consciousness of their unimpeachable objectivity and of their great parsimony and power. And yet the structuralist attention to Aristotelian analogy—summed up in the famous if confounding formula of mediation and transformation, $f_x(a)$: $f_y(b)$ :: $f_x(b)$: $f_{a-1}(y)$—teaches us something important about symbolic thought and about the inchoate from which it arises. It teaches that symbolic activity and hence symbolic inquiry is essentially the relating of domains of experience and the study of the relational equivalence of the arrangement of entities in these domains. We confront the inchoate in another way here in recognizing that in respect to symbols, we do not understand things in and of themselves. Symbolic understanding is understanding that is obtained by extension of our attention to something else which is more familiar.

This is not to say very much, perhaps, because what else do we mean by the phrase "to symbolize" than to let something stand for something else. (I should add here that I have had a long standing

---

[2] Diamond points up the inconsistency in the "presumably highly symbolic categories of structuralism and the reductionism inherent in its explanatory principle" (1974:302). It is the reduction of the symbolic to the banal symbolic function.

objection to the symbol concept as at once so unitary and polysemic itself as not to reveal satisfactorily those processes by which, in objectified thought, more familiar and concrete objects are related to inchoate subjects—processes by which domains are related to each.) And yet since empiricism would hold to the view that we understand most clearly that which we observe most directly it is worth pointing out that structuralism teaches that we understand not by exclusive intense and unflinching attention to the subject of interest but by allowing for the eye to wander, searching out an interaction of it in other domains of experience. Levi-Strauss's series, *Mythologiques,* would offer very feeble understanding if it focused on one or several myths only. It is by bringing into play many different myths so that their relational structures can interact that our understanding is enhanced.

I do not wish to necessarily profess adherence to the abstract principles and mental categories, the unwelcome contradictions such as being both born of one and of two or being of both nature and culture, that Levi-Strauss adduces as the real referents of the objectified thought, the concrete things conglomerated by bricolage, that he studies. By the lights of my own field experience there is a jump in the production of these principles which makes me uneasy about them. One worries that they are more a product of Western academic preoccupations and categories than of the local thought in which they are embedded.

But I do wish to adhere to the structural strategy of understanding its materials by indirections—by recognizing that some domains of experience are more familiar and some more inchoate, the latter often the ones most focal to our interest. Symbolic thought brings the one to bear on the other. And even if we cannot readily differentiate between inchoate and familiar domains of experience, the central place of analogic thought and relational understanding in the structural approach— its strategic employ of the devices of the savage mind in studying the products of the savage mind, which is to say allowing oneself to be "thought of" by the materials themselves—gives it particular depth of penetration where symbolic constructions are concerned. This strategy brings us particularly close to those forms of explanation—proverbial wisdom we might call it—which are much more widespread in the world and surely in the anthropological data than the canons of discursive reasoning would lead us to believe. (This general point has been made succinctly by J. Maquet, 1974.) It is, as well, a strategy that points us towards the way that culture coheres: by the resonance between the relational structures of different domains of experience.

Our epigraph from Van Gennep now gives this part of our argument away—at least as far as our discipline is concerned. For we recognize how prevalent the house metaphor has been in our professional formulations—in our attempts to convincingly understand the inchoate experience of change and passage through the life cycle. The more directly we look at social life, perhaps, the more we are impelled to see it in other terms. We have familiarized our subject by bringing to bear one of the most familiar domains of experience—houselife—and in that, we have created a central and recurrent image of our social thought. It is not the only familiar domain to which we have turned to make our subject matter more satisfyingly intelligible. The game metaphor—social life is a game and we are all familiar with games—has long been beguiling. The drama metaphor—social life is a drama and we are all familiar with dramas and with being dramatic—has as long been compelling. And now we have the text metaphor—and what could be more familiar and persuasive to a text building animal like the academic one—which promises because of the moribund quality of the other metaphors perhaps—which is to say, the decline of the shock of recognition contained in them through overuse—to restore to us now a finally adequate explanation, justifying, indeed compelling, a new campaign of inquiry. We will bend the inchoate to our purposes at last.

4

"I must be getting somewhere
near the center of the earth."

(Alice speculating as she is
falling down the rabbit hole.)

The objectified thought or the objective correlatives of social science inquiry propel us away from the center of gravity of our particular argument here—an argument whose principal ideas we have been teasing out of their embeddedness in the dark at the bottom of the stairs. Let us return once more to our particular "fascinans."[3]

Recently we have been working among mountain cattle-keepers in northern Spain. These people, like many of the cattle-keeping countrymen of Europe, characteristically live above the stable. (It's a marvelous energy-saving arrangement, by the way.) The dark at the bottom of the stairs is the stable itself—and it is dark even at midday for the stable door is small and usually closed and there is but one small nether window. It is a hermetic environment heavy with the acrid odor of animals and animal wastes barely sweetened by the smell of hay. It is not only animal wastes. Until quite recent "improvements" in village life, the stable was used by humans as well.

For the urban visitor with little appreciation for animals or for the ultimate good uses of manure, the atmosphere is daunting. But for the villagers it is redolent with much, if not all, that is most meaningful to them. Or how else could it be that a villager could fling wide the stable door and turn to the visitor wɪth the exclamation: "Ye un paraiso verda!" All the visitor can make out in the obscurity is the white muzzles of six or seven cows turned with vague curiosity toward the light which is itself reflected in a row of large, patient, luminescent eyes.

[3] One has in mind Rudolf Otto's discussion of the core mystery of life—unfathomable, paradoxical, and antinomic—which he treats both as a "mysterium tremendum," that is to say, an object of awesome contemplation, and as a "fascinans," something which impels man to do something about it. I hope it's clear that we treat the inchoate here as a "fascinans," *not* as a "mysterium tremendum" (see Otto 1923).

Even more at night does the stable become a part of family life. The family is attentive to the signs rising from the dark below: the shifting of weight, the rubbing of a flank against a post, the signs of the laborious bedding down, an unexpected bovine cough or eructation, and even the sound of a new calf suckling. One senses that the family is about as attentive to these nether regions as they are to their own visceral processes—quite without considering that their own visceral processes eventuate in the stable. A house without a ruminating, rumbling, wheezing shifting stable is a moribund house and, in fact, during the day or during the summer months when the cows are out or up upon the steep meadows the house is only half a house, its peristalsis suspended and the life of the inhabitants projected out upon the streets and plazas and up upon the high meadows.

The reader will now see what I am about here and what this mountain housing has made us aware of: that if for Van Gennep society can be a house (of whose basement, however, we empiricists have to constantly remind ourselves), so for many peoples the body can be a house and the dark at the bottom of the stairs can assume visceral cloacal genitive functions. (I am sure we were all vaguely aware of this even without the case of these countrymen.) These are the functions from which we, in all our urbanity, avert our eyes. But the countryman, a more natural man, looks directly at them seeing in them the sources of his well being, the fertility of his fields, the marketable wealth of his patrimony, the very replica and repository of his vitality. The manger—we can understand it if we try—is his salvation and his paradise.

In symbolic inquiry the body and its multitudinous processes must be always present though just how it is present, for reasons of our impulse toward aversion and repression, we are never quite certain. Such things are most often deeply embedded and cloaked over with a seemly obscurity. Periodically throughout his career Kenneth Burke, who has so often played the devil's advocate to the literary sensibility and the literary establishment, has sought to whip off that cloak and discover evidence in even the most heroic, the most noble, and the most exalted texts of what he calls the cathartic function or the Demonic Trinity: the three purgative outlets of the *parties honteuses* (see Burke 1966). The hidden sources of this cathartic imagery give it its power, he argues, and putting one's finger upon it is always ticklish, often tedious, and occasionally intolerable. Indeed we have learned from the early years of Freudian interpretation where everything was turned into Phallic symbols just how tedious such interpretation could be.

But I do not want our possible perturbations over such interpretations to deflect us from that dark arena of our interest where thought emerges from non-thought—where ideas arise out of that embedded condition in which we so often find them in anthropological work. For anthropologists, exegesis is the exception not the rule in contrast with life in the academies where ideas grow on trees, are in the air, and are trodden underfoot. As academics we tend too much to take ideas for granted as if they were always there—there before us as, in fact, they are in the synopticons of the literary tradition. Symbolic inquiry recognizes how embedded ideas are in images and objects—among these the body—and how poorly understood are the procedures by which ideas are appropriately squeezed from their embedded condition. That is part of the inchoateness of our inquiry. We have already expressed misgivings here about the abstract ideas which Levi-Strauss finds to be the referents of the concrete thought he examines, and I have elsewhere worried about the imposition of "imageless ideas" in anthropological inquiry (Fernandez 1978). I worried that a great deal of what we were researching was already defined or presented to us in cognitive terms before the research began, and that our field materials were being fitted pseudo-conceptually to our preconceptions. We could be surer of our authenticity if we would anchor ourselves in local images—and that may be perhaps the main strategy for dealing with the inchoate.

Still, the relationship between symbols, images, and ideas is difficult. No one should pretend otherwise. Take the central symbol of these village stables: the cow. I wish I could easily say what the idea or ideas of the cow are to these villagers who are so fascinated by them. As an ethnographer, one is tempted to paraphrase Tennyson: Bovid in the stable stall, If I could understand what you are, I would understand the universe and all. There are words, of course, to attach to cows—plenty of them. And there are images of cows that one can elicit. But village "thinking" about the cow goes on largely embedded at a deeper level where bodily states of contentment and discontent, desire or satiety, extension and distention are experienced in relation to the cow. They know the cow much more that way than in relation to the emergent cognitive apparatus employed in the object world. That is to say that what Langer (1951) has described as the "symbolic transformation of experience" takes place at a very deep and obscure (one almost slips and says obscene) level having to do with bodily states presented in that symbolism. This profound organismic organization, if it is an organization, is characteristic of, in Langer's terms, presentational symbolism. It is a symbolism which achieves an ordering of experience a stage earlier—we would say here, a floor deeper—than discursive thought. Discursive thought may be applied to that symbolism as a system of ideas, but it cannot be as deeply associated with it. And unless such thought itself emerges out of that deeper organization, it risks not being associated with it at all—pseudo-conceptualization, as it were. The strategy for coping with these difficulties, the strategy of pseudo-conceptualization by readymade interpretation, was convincingly rejected by Freud almost from the first part of his argument in *The Interpretation of Dreams* (1955). Let the dreams themselves be fully heard and told and seen before we begin our analysis.

But in respect to the matters we are seeking here to bring out, Jung may be the better guide. Jung (1959) frequently argued that ideas emerge into mental form from physiological remoteness and out of "undifferentiated totalities"—by which Jung meant the condensation characteristic of the symbol. He wrote that "symbols of the self arise in the depths of the body and they express its materiality as much as the structure of the perceiving consciousness." One does not have to accept Jung's notion of the archetype nor of the archaic unconscious to recognize the importance of this view. The psychologist D.W. Harding in a perceptive treatment of "The Hinterland of Thought," finds Jung's views of these deep processes valuable with the exception of his notion that the image archetype itself arises from the remote depths of the body. What Harding says of the horse symbol is apposite to these villagers' attachment to cows:

For instance some sense of surging animal vitality and its huge potential power may arise in any of us and may emerge into conscious experience from below, in the way that the experience of hunger emerges out of bodily processes. As it comes towards "symbolic transformation" the most appropriate image to hand may be, or may have been for many centuries past, the horse; and the horse may then serve as the symbol of a very complex mass of inarticulate potential experience, including a sense of the delight, the danger, the power, the vulnerability, the wildness and the manageableness of animal vitality. But although the meaning of the symbol may have come towards definition out of the remotenesses of the whole psychosomatic person, the image— the horse—seems most likely to have entered by way of the sensory surfaces, especially the eye. [Harding 1960:21.]

Just so. The image of the cow—which, of course, has a different set of valences than the horse—comes to the villagers as it does not come to the urban dweller, out of their daily experience. But presented there, it is taken down to be associated with the deepest physiological awareness of repletion, evacuation, nurturance, and satiety. Above all, the cow is a symbol of satiety.

These matters are so inchoate that one despairs of getting one's ideas about them correctly put. The more we focus upon them the more they recede before us and the more we are driven elsewhere to other domains for such clarification as lies in metaphor and the argument of images. Harding recognizes this problem. And he has produced a notable master metaphor in which to embed his ideas. We may quote it as a useful contrast to the master metaphor we have been arguing here:

We are still obliged to use similes and metaphors in describing these things, and I think the metaphor of distance as well as depth is needed. We stand at the harbour of our mind and watch flotillas of ideas far out at sea coming up over the horizon, already in formation of a sort; and though we can reorder them to a great extent on their closer approach, we cannot disregard the organization they had before they came in sight. They are all submarines, partly under water the whole time and capable of submerging entirely at any point and being lost to sight until analytic techniques undo the repression. But it constitutes a fundamental difference whether an idea is out of mind because it has been forced to dive or because it has not yet come up over the horizon. Sometimes repressed ideas may be close in-shore. . . . Others may be both under water and at a great distance; they find expression in some sorts of dreaming. . . . And in creative work great numbers of ideas, more or less organized, are simply out of sight beyond the horizon and can be brought into view only through the redispositions we make amongst the in-shore mental shipping that we *can* see and control. [Harding 1960:19–20.]

Would we not without such similes fall, like Alice, irremediably to the very center of our experience where we would have no perspective whatsoever? It is that fear of falling into the abyss that more than anything else, perhaps, energizes the analogies that are the first step in our climb toward cognition and our emergence into the realm of ideas. In the face of the inchoate, the first strategy is the argument of images. We cope by such versimilitude, even if it only be by wishing that in a situation of profound dilemma we were a Kellogg's cornflake floating in a bowl taking movies, relaxing awhile, living in style. Reflecting in that image will give us plenty of ideas about the normless situation of the student generation during the Vietnam War.

5

"La vida es sueño."

Calderon de la Barca

In some respects this paper—this argument of images—in its rhetorical quality has had the air of an epistle to the South Californians

seeking to excite their moral imaginations, to bring about some conversion in them. It's a normal impulse experienced by Bible Belters
in Elysian climes. But we are not untrue to our subject because symbolic
activity is mostly rhetorical, seeking to convert self and others to other
notions of things. And symbolic constructions are worlds in which it
is hoped the converted can live, if only for an imaginary moment. Any
inquiry into symbols must recognize the conversion and conviction that
lies in them—they move us in quality space. The particular quality
space we have been exploring here by means of a sequence of symbols
is a dark environment, close and heavily charged. The claims of the
object world prevent extensive sojourns but it would be a mistake to
ignore the particular coalescences taking place there however obscure—
or its everpresence.

Elsewhere in my particular approach to symbolism—I prefer the
technical term sign-image—I have sought to, by a discursive effort,
distinguish signal activity from symbolic activity, social consensus
from cultural consensus. I have sought to follow through the harmonic
permutations of syntax and paradigm. I have argued that metaphor-
metonymic progressions have a predictability within cultures—and that
they are culture-specific. This has all been mainfloor analysis. It's a
different thing to turn to things subterranean—where one must turn
perforce to the argument of images.

Now an objectionable thing occurs—at least to a pragmatic, civic-
minded people—when we turn our attention to the dark at the bottom
of the stairs. It begins to claim a primacy, exert an exclusive and
indulgent fascination. We sense that it risks turning the world upside
down. And here the play by that master dramatist of the *Siglo de Oro,*
Calderon, comes to mind. *La vida es sueño* is a play that espouses
that tendency present in the Mediterranean world since Plato's cave,
and surely pervasive in Iberian eschatological thought, to devalue the
things of this world as imperfect and confused and transient—like a
dream. In its somber and more philosophic moments, it is the tragic
view of life.

Science is not only pragmatic and civic-minded—it is also, essentially, robustly optimistic. The consequences of its activity may be
tragic but its cast of mind is surely not. Such a cast of mind is bound

to be uncomfortable in the presence of such deep fascinations as we have been exploring here. What is the good of such explorations? What responsibility to the management of the social order and the preparation of a brighter future is present in it? One remembers those insinuating phrases in that piece of Vietnam popular culture we introduced to begin with, "Punky's Dilemma"—a song like so many songs of the period about the larger civic responsibility, about the social order, and about the light at the end of the tunnel:

> Old Roger draft-dodger [it goes]
> Leavin' by the basement door,
> Everybody knows what he's
> Tippy-toeing down there for.

And yet Calderon's play—all his plays—if not about social order is surely about social solidarity, about collective responsibility, and about the limitation of personal visions. But Calderon's cast of mind, and this is, perhaps, a predominant strain in the Spanish mentality since the Golden Age and the collapse of the empire, can place no great confidence in devotion to the material and social advantages of life—to the pragmatics. For Calderon the only guide is renunciation of personal advantage. So the tragic view of life envisions a basis for social order and enduring solidarity—even if it is that of the "last best hope" variety. It is enough, perhaps, to stimulate moral imaginations with the comparative possibilities for social solidarity and social order contained in a tragic, world-renouncing, darkness-obsessed view on the one hand and an optimistic, strategic-minded, world-embracing view on the other. But it cannot, at least for an anthropologist, be assumed out of hand that a preoccupation with the dark at the bottom of the stairs negates *everything* we hold most dear!

In the end here I am myself too much committed to the pragmatic optimism of my generation—to the sunny side of the Bible Belt—to leave a reader pondering the tragic path to social order and conviviality, leave her or him with only a stimulated moral imagination or an indignant one as the case may be. There is an additional and very practical reason why the inchoate should interest us. It is, very simply, the matrix of those revitalized images which enable cultures to regroup themselves and live on a bit. Perhaps because of our commitments to the tenor of normal life we tend to be preoccupied in the social sciences with the more or less smooth coordinations of signal behaviors, with common sense understandings, and with the strategic management of the object world. We hold the inchoate in abeyance. But we anthropologists above all, because we have seen it so many times, know how quickly a society can be precipitated into anomie, the normal state of daily life in the world out there brought to a halt. It is then that the central nervous system, which has been held in abeyance in the normal routine, reasserts its reality and men and women return to deeper levels of experience to find images and symbols to live with, and live by (see Fischer 1971). At any rate, for an anthropologist like myself who has spent his life studying revitalization movements, the importance of these deeper levels in the generation of revitalized culture is understandable. Most of the movements I studied in Africa began in an extended dream or vision. In a very real sense "su cultura es sueño."

And perhaps it is not only the culture of revitalization movements. Perhaps the method we must follow to understand the coherence of any culture in the most comprehensive sense is little different from the method employed by Freud in understanding the coherence of dreams: identification of elements, tracing their overdetermination out to their superabundant associations, and finally synthesizing underlying themes (see Foulkes 1978). Or why would one of the most stimulating collections of recent years (Geertz 1973) be named so precisely after the master's work: *The Interpretation* (not of dreams but) *of Cultures?*

POSTSCRIPT

In lively discussion at the UCLA Department after this paper was read, I was pressed to be more specific and didactic. A problem with the argument of images, of course, is that ideas—the currency of academic life—are often embedded and not explicit. Academic auditors want, quite naturally, useful—that is, negotiable—results. Let me therefore be explicit here about 1) the definition of the inchoate and 2) the strategies for coping with it.

By the inchoate we mean the underlying (psychophysiological) and overlying (sociocultural) sense of entity (entirety of being or wholeness) which we reach for to express (by predication) and act out (by performance) but can never grasp. Hence frustration is constant and predication is recurrent. The wholeness of the inchoate is complicated and obscured by such dilemmas, paradoxes, and ambiguities as a) the duplicity of language, b) role conflict in social life, c) the idiosyncracies of experience and its interpretation, etc.

As regards the difference between the inchoate and the unconscious, it should be said that the former term seeks to be a concept pointing at the systematic intersection of the sociocultural and the psychophysiological. It is a concept that seeks to suggest the ultimate undefinability of this sociocultural-personal wholeness but it is a concept which locates in that ultimate undefinability the "fascinans" that is the impulse to recurrent predication and performance.

It follows that there are certain strategies for coping with the inchoate, at once undefinable *and* impulsive: a) we should not begin with imageless inquiry but we should consider first the images predicated upon the inchoate and in which a culture's idea system is embedded; b) we should recognize the polyvalence—overdetermination—of that which issues from the inchoate and the centrality of ambiguity; c) we should recognize the temporal quality of any interpretation—its idiosyncrasy of time, place, and person; d) we should recognize the relational quality of such coherence analogic reason is able to assign to the inchoate and the indirection of such intelligence, which always confirms itself in other domains. There are several strategies to be avoided: the adversarial strategy, the essentialist strategy, and the direct-inspection strategy.

Anthropological colleagues were kind enough to provide me with their associations to the "Dark" image. The readiness of their response and its diversity proves the resonance of the image in our culture and its multivocality. Here is a sampling:

"The dark was my father's incompetence—or at least that sump pump that he could never fix," or "It's me lying in bed and worrying that some door on the first floor was open to the burglars of our family wellbeing," or "It was illicit adolescent love-making with an ear tuned to family stirrings above," or "To me it's all these neighbor's children who had disappeared and might be in our basement, our skeletons, as well as any others," or "It once was for me musty barely growing things or preserved things—roots, apples, potatoes, comestibles—in the cellar, but now it's a rumpus room or a music room or a washer-dryer and a humming heater—not very dark at all."

ACKNOWLEDGEMENTS

Thanks to Hildred Geertz and Buck Schieffelin for prodding me to concentrate my attention on the "inchoate." To Nancy Schwartz special thanks for, once again, bringing her frame of reference to bear on a particular problem with such fertility. And to various colleagues—professional privilege prohibits me from naming them—who have free-associated so readily to the "Dark at the Bottom of the Stairs."

REFERENCES

Beildeman, Thomas O.
    1980   The Moral Imagination of the Kaguru: Some Thoughts on Tricksters. *American Ethnologist,* 7(1):27–42.

Burke, Kenneth
    1966   Mind, Body and the Unconscious; The Thinking of the Body; and *Somnia Ad Urinandum.* In *Language in Symbolic Action:* essays on life, literature, and method. Berkeley: University of California Press, pp. 63–80, 308–343, 344–358.

Christie, Agatha
    1976   *Sleeping Murder.* New York: Bantam.

Diamond, Stanley
    1974   The Myth of Structuralism. In *The Unconscious in Culture,* ed. by Ino Rossi. New York: Dutton, pp. 292–335.

Fernandez, James W.
    1975   On the Concept of the Symbol. *Current Anthropology,* 16(4):652–654.

    1975a   On Reading the Sacred into the Profane: The Dramatic Fallacy in the Work of Victor Turner. *Journal for the Scientific Study of Religion,* 14:191–197.

    1978   Imageless Ideas in African Inquiry. Paper read at SSRC–ACLS Conference on Cultural Transformations in Africa, January 1978, at the Smithsonian Conference Center, Maryland.

Fischer, R.
    1971   A Cartography of the Ecstatic and Meditative States. *Science,* 174:897–904.

Foulkes, David
    1978   *A Grammar of Dreams.* New York: Basic Books.

Freud, Sigmund
  1955   *The Interpretation of Dreams*. Orig. 1900. New York: Basic
          Books.

Geertz, Clifford
  1973   *The Interpretation of Cultures*. New York: Basic Books.

  1977   Found in Translation: On the Social History of the Moral
          Imagination. *The Georgia Review,* 31:788–810.

Harding, D.W.
  1960   The Hinterland of Thought. In *Metaphor and Symbol,* ed.
          by L.C. Knights and Basil Cottle. London: Butterworths,
          pp. 10–23.

Inge, William
  1958   *The Dark at the Top of the Stairs*. New York: Random
          House.

Jakobson, Roman
  n.d.   Shifters, verbal categories and the Russian verb. In *Russian
          language project,* Cambridge, pp. 1–14.

Jung, C.G.
  1959   *The Archetypes and the Collective Unconscious*. Trans. by
          R.F.C. Hill. New York: Pantheon.

  1963   *Memories, Dreams, and Reflections*. London: Collins.

Langer, Susan
  1951   *Philosophy in a New Key*. London: Seeker.

LeGuin, Ursula Kroeber
  1975   *The Tombs of Atuan*. New York: Bantam.

Levi-Strauss, Claude
  1955   *Tristes Tropiques*. Paris: Plon.

Maquet, Jacques
  1974   Isomorphism and Symbolism as "Explanations" in the
          Analysis of Myths. In *The Unconscious in Culture,* ed. by
          Ino Rossi. New York: Dutton, pp. 107–122.

Otto, Roudlof
   1923   *The Idea of the Holy.* London: Oxford University Press.

Thomas, L.L., J.Z. Kronenfeld, and D.B. Kronenfeld
   1976   Asdiwal Crumbles: A Critique of Levi-Straussian Myth
           Analysis. *American Ethnologist,* 3(1): 147–174.

COLLECTIVE REPRESENTATIONS AND MENTAL REPRESENTATIONS IN RELIGIOUS SYMBOL SYSTEMS

Melford E. Spiro

In this paper I want to address the relationship between statements of the following two types: "The omnipotence of God is a basic doctrine of Christianity," and, "As a Christian, John holds the doctrine of the omnipotence of God to be true." To put it more abstractly, I want to address the relationship between religious doctrines as they are found in the collective representations of a social group, on the one hand, and in the mental representations of the religious actors, on the other. Divested of jargon, I want to ask why it is that religious actors believe in the doctrines that comprise the religious system of their culture. If this question seems trivial, or if the answer seems obvious, it is only because we have for too long—certainly since Durkheim—accepted the coercive power of cultural symbols on the human mind to be a self-evident truth.

I have at the outset introduced the mind as one of the key terms of our discussion because one of the unexamined assumptions of much of anthropology is that any attempt to understand culture by reference to the mind is at best to confuse levels of analysis, if not levels of 'reality,' and at worst, to perpetuate the intellectual sin of reductionism. Although I oppose the confusion and abjure the sin, I will argue that inasmuch as cultural doctrines, ideas, values, and the like exist in the minds of social actors—where else *could* they exist?—to attempt to understand culture by ignoring the human mind is like attempting to understand *Hamlet* by ignoring the Prince of Denmark. To be sure, cultural doctrines and the like are encoded in those public and visible signs (cultural symbols) which, following Durkheim, we call 'collective representations'; but since the latter neither possess nor announce their meanings, they must be found in the minds of social actors. If this is not so, then to understand culture it is not sufficient to attend to cultural symbol systems and how they work; it is also necessary to attend to the mind and how *it* works. That, at any rate, is the thesis I wish to explore in this paper.

In referring to the mind, I am not only referring to those intellectual and information-processing functions which are often exclusively associated with that concept. Rather, I am referring to all of those psychological processes—cognitive, affective, and motivational—which underlie any type of complex behavior. Such a broad notion of 'mind' is especially important if we are to deal adequately with the complex problem with which we are concerned in this paper. Its complexity is a function of the fact that although religious systems are cognitive systems, they persist because of powerful motivational dispositions and affective needs of the social actors to which they are responsive. Moreover, although the culturally constituted meanings of the symbols in which religious doctrines are encoded are consciously held by the actors, the latter also invest them with private, often unconscious meanings, whose cognitive salience is no less important for their understanding. This being the case, in order to explain why social actors believe in the religious doctrines of their culture we must attend to the motivational and affective, as well as the cognitive properties of the mind; and in attending to these properties, we must be concerned with their unconscious, as well as their conscious dimensions.

In an important sense, this paper may be viewed as a long, and somewhat extended and delayed commentary on an observation I made eleven years ago as a discussant at a symposium on symbolic anthropology. "If symbolic behavior is even half as important as Freud, for example, suggested, symbolic anthropology is the custodian of the richest of all the mines which are worked by the science of man. To be sure, we have not yet produced our Freud, but until we do, perhaps we would be wise to reread *The Interpretation of Dreams*" (Spiro 1969:214).

1

Before embarking on this inquiry, I should perhaps define its basic terms. By "belief" I will mean any proposition concerning human beings, society, and the world that is held to be true. By "religious belief" I will mean any belief that, directly or indirectly, relates to beings who possess greater power than human beings and animals, with whom human beings sustain asymmetrical relationships (inter-actions and transactions), and who affect human lives for good or for ill. In short, "religious" beliefs comprise that sub-set of beliefs which, directly or indirectly, are concerned with 'superhuman' beings. Not all beliefs, of course, are culturally-constituted, and since the distinguishing feature of "culture," as I shall use that term, is tradition, a "culturally-constituted" belief—religious or any other—is a *traditional* belief. That is, it is one which is acquired by learning a cultural doctrine—a proposition about man, society, or nature—that originates and develops in the history of a social group, and is transmitted from generation to generation by means of those social processes that are denoted by such terms as "education" and "enculturation." Our definition of "symbol" will be deferred until later.

With these definitions in mind, and considering what I have already said about the need to study culture in its relationship to the social actors—the culture-bearers, as they used to be called—the investigation of a culturally-constituted belief involves—or at least it ought to involve—a six-fold task. First, the cultural doctrine which is the basis for the belief must be described. Second, its traditional meanings must be ascertained. Third, its relationship to the other doctrines comprising the system of which it is a part must be delineated. Fourth, the structure of the system must be explicated. Fifth, the grounds for the actors' accepting the doctrine as their own belief must be uncovered. Finally, the functions of holding this belief—the consequences, for either the social actors or their society—must be discovered.

In referring above to the "meanings" of cultural doctrines, I was, of course, speaking elliptically; for their meanings, as I have already said, are "located" not in the doctrines themselves, but in the minds of the actors who hold and transmit them. Thus, when we ask, "what does the Christian doctrine in the omnipotence of God mean?" we are really asking, "what does this doctrine mean to Christians?" But since cultural doctrines are acquired through social transmission (rather than constructed from personal experience), the answer to questions of this type is far from obvious, as it depends on the cognitive salience with which the doctrines are acquired as personal beliefs.

Briefly, and in ascending order of importance, we may delineate a hierarchy comprising five levels of cognitive salience. (a) The actors *learn about* the doctrines; as Bertrand Russell would say, they acquire an "acquaintance" with them. (b) The actors not only learn about the doctrines, but they also *understand* their traditional meanings as they are interpreted in authoritative texts, for example, or by recognized specialists. (c) The actors not only understand the traditional meanings of the doctrines, but understanding them, they *believe* that the doctrines so defined are true, correct, or right. That actors hold a doctrine to be true does not in itself, however, indicate that it importantly effects the manner in which they conduct their lives. Hence (d) at the fourth level of cognitive salience, cultural doctrines are not only held to be true, but they inform the behavioral environment of social actors, serving to structure their perceptual worlds and, consequently, to *guide* their actions. When cultural doctrines are acquired at this level we may say that they are genuine beliefs, rather than cultural clichés. (e) As genuine beliefs the doctrines not only guide, but they also serve to *instigate* action; they possess motivational as well as cognitive properties. Thus, one who has acquired, for example, the doctrine of hell at this—the fifth—level of cognitive salience, not only incorporates this doctrine as part of his cosmography, but he also internalizes it as part of his motivational system; it arouses strong affect (anxiety) which, in turn, motivates him to action whose purpose is the avoidance of hell.

Although, in general, anthropologists have assumed that cultural doctrines are acquired at the fourth, if not the fifth level of this hierarchy, this assumption is all too often unwarranted, and it has led to erroneous interpretations of the importance of particular cultural doctrines, as well as to extravagant claims concerning the importance of culture in general in human affairs. Thus, for example, many key features of the social structure, political system, and economic organization of the Buddhist societies of Southeast Asia have often been explained as a function of the putative 'otherworldly' orientation of Buddhist actors, an orientation which is inferred from the Buddhist doctrine of nirvana. This explanation, however, is typically invalid because, as recent anthropological studies of these societies have shown, except for a few monastic virtuosi, this doctrine has not been internalized by Buddhist actors as a culturally-constituted belief, but is rather a cultural cliché.

My point, then, is that in order to explain a cultural doctrine—that is to account for its existence—we must first interpret it; we must discover its 'meaning' for the actors. This requires that we ascertain at which of the five levels of cognitive salience adumbrated above it has been acquired as a belief. On the premise that cultural doctrines have been acquired as personal beliefs at the fourth or fifth level of that hierarchy, anthropologists have typically adopted two complementary intellectual modes in their attempts to explain and interpret them. One mode is concerned with culturally particular analysis and the other with trans-cultural analysis.

Conceived in the first mode, the analysis of cultural beliefs focuses on the local ethnographic setting in all of its uniqueness. For this mode, the question of why the Burmese, say, believe in cultural doctrines related to gods, demons, and the Buddha evokes an unambiguous answer: as part of the cultural heritage of their society, these doctrines have been acquired as beliefs by each successive generation of Burmese from previous generations. Hence, this mode is especially interested in discovering how these doctrines are related to other aspects of Burmese culture and society such that, together, they comprise an integrated "system." To the extent that this mode presses its analysis further, it turns in one of two directions. One direction, culture history, is concerned with diachronic 'explanation,' and attempts to discover the socio-economic and political conditions which might have led to the invention or borrowing of these doctrines. The other, symbolic anthropology, is concerned with symbolic 'interpretation,' and attempts to discover the meanings of the symbols by means of which the Burmese express and represent their doctrines. In both cases, anthropologists who operate exclusively in this mode usually contend that cultural beliefs can be understood only in the historical context and the conceptual terms of the culture in which they are embedded. For, so they claim, in as much as the history which produced them and the symbols which represent them are unique, their meanings cannot be conveyed non-trivially by trans-cultural concepts.

The analysis of cultural beliefs conceived in the second mode goes beyond the first mode in that it seeks explanations not only of a culturally parochial, but also of a trans-cultural provenance. This mode is necessary to explain certain phenomena which are difficult, if not impossible to explain in the first mode. Why, to take one example, do cultural doctrines sometimes die out or are sufficiently transformed over time as to become unrecognizable? Or, to take another example, why are some cultural beliefs no more than clichés, while others are held with strong conviction and emotional intensity? In the second mode, explanations for such questions are usually not sought in parochial culture history, but in generic human experience. Moreover, those analysts who employ the second, as well as the first mode, usually disagree with the contention of those who employ the first mode exclusively that the cross-cultural diversity in symbols and symbol systems implies that the meanings of cultural beliefs are unique and incommensurable. They contend, rather, that underlying the wide range of variability in the 'surface' meanings of cultural symbols, there is a narrow range of variability—if not universality—at some 'deep' level of meaning, and that their interpretation must attend to the latter, as well as the former, meanings.

Since it is this second intellectual mode whose application to the analysis of religious symbol systems I wish to explore in this paper, it is necessary to examine the set of assumptions—at least as I see them—on which it rests. First, despite the diversity of human cultures, the minds of culture-bearers everywhere share pan-human characteristics ("psychic unity of mankind"); second, these characteristics are the product of a shared biological phylogeny, on the one hand, and a similar social ontogeny on the other; third, the diversity of cultures represents variable attempts of the human mind to cope with the existential and adaptive problems of individual and social living, which vary as a function of diverse historical experiences and ecological conditions; fourth, the diversity which is found at the 'surface' meanings of cultural beliefs is associated with pan-human regularities in their 'deep' meanings; fifth, these regularities are transformed, by processes to be described below, into the historically conditioned, and therefore culturally parochial, meanings of the symbols by which these beliefs are represented and conveyed. It is primarily in their surface meanings that the much heralded diversity and relativity of human cultures, whose proclamation has become the hallmark of anthropology, is to be found.

Just as the first mode in the study of cultural beliefs can be divided into culture history and symbolic anthropology, the second mode can likewise be divided into two types: structuralism and culture-and-personality. Structuralism, whose founder and most eminent figure is Levi-Strauss, is wholly concerned with the cognitive, and more particularly, the intellectual dimension of the psychic unity of mankind. Hence, it views the resolution of intellectual puzzles and paradoxes as the crucial feature of the mind, so far, at least, as its relationship to religious beliefs and mythic themes is concerned. In their interpretation of myth, for example, structuralists not only can (and do) ignore all other characteristics of the mind, but they also exclude from their purview the social actors who acquire and transmit the myths, focusing their attention on the myths themselves, as they are recorded in texts.

Culture-and-personality theory, insofar at least, as it takes its departure from the psychoanalytic conception of the mind, is concerned not only with the intellectual dimension of cognition, but also with its other dimensions, as well as with the affective characteristics of the mind. Given these concerns, it holds that the investigation of religion and myth must focus as much on the psychological characteristics of the social actors, as on the structural characteristics of religion and myth, in order to arrive at an adequate interpretation and explanation for them. It is this approach to religion that I shall explicate in this paper. First, however, we must delineate those characteristics of the mind that are relevant for understanding religious symbols.

2

That human beings attempt to maximize pleasure, and that pleasure involves the gratification of needs, wishes, and desires—whether these be biological, social, emotional, or intellectual—are two propositions concerning the human mind which, I take it, would evoke fairly wide assent. That, typically, wishes and desires can be gratified only by transactions with the external environment—both physical and social— and that these transactions are based on specifiable perceptual and mental processes whose characteristics are universal are also (I expect) widely accepted assumptions. Thus, with respect to perceptual processes, if there ever was a society whose members could never distinguish fantasy from reality, or hallucinatory from veridical perception, such a society, surely, is part of the fossil record of human history. The same consideration holds with respect to mental processes. Societies whose members were typically unable to assess causal relationships, to grasp logical connections, to construct valid inductive generalizations, or to make valid deductive inferences—these are societies in which even the simplest of subsistence activities would have little chance of success. In a word, such societies would not have survived.

The perceptual and mental processes alluded to above—which, taken jointly, I shall label as "cognitive"—comprise a type (in the Weberian sense) in which mentation is governed by normally accepted rules of logic, and in which ideas and thoughts are represented by *verbal* signs which are combined and manipulated by conventional rules of grammar and syntax. It is a type, moreover, in which the perception of internal stimuli is distinguished from that of external stimuli. In the study of dreams, fantasy, and related phenomena, however, we encounter yet another type of cognition. So far as mentation is concerned, it is a type in which ideas and thoughts are typically represented by *visual* signs (both iconic and symbolic) and whose logic, as we shall see below, is analogous to that exhibited in metaphor, metonymy, and other tropes. So far as perception is concerned, it is a type in which stimuli originating in the inner world are taken as objects and events in the outer world. Following Freud, this type may be termed the "primary process" mode of cognition, in contrast to the first type which may be termed the "secondary process" mode.

In this paper, we shall be primarily concerned with the primary process mode of cognition. For if, to turn from the individual to the sociocultural level, economic and technological systems, for example, may be said to be based more-or-less on the secondary process mode, then I would claim that mythico-religious and ritual systems are based to a much greater extent on the primary process mode. In considering the above discussion of the latter mode, this claim means, first, that religion and myth possess a logical structure which differs importantly from that found in the technico-economic domain, strictly conceived; second, it means that they are the cultural domains, *par excellence,* in which fantasy is taken for reality. In short, they are the domains in which the adaptive constraints on the satisfaction of wishes and desires find an important exception. We shall begin this discussion with the second claim, deferring the discussion of the first to the following section.

To better understand the claim that in religion and myth fantasy is taken for reality, it is instructive to compare these cultural phenomena with dreams; those psychological phenomena in which this dimension of the primary process is most obvious and best understood. The dream world is a *reified* world. That is, although dreams consist of images of persons and events, these images are believed by the dreamer to *be,* rather than to *represent,* the persons and events they signify. In short, in the dream the mental representation of a thing is taken for the thing itself. Similarly, based on culturally acquired religious doctrines and rituals, as well as mythic narratives, the religious believer constructs a mental representation—also in the form of images—of a special and wondrous world of beings and events. Unlike the dreamer, however, the religious believer does not confuse the mythico-religious world with his mental representation of it. Except in trance and other altered states of consciousness, the images in his mind, as well as the cultural symbols from which they are constructed, are not believed to *constitute* the beings and events that comprise that world; rather, they are believed to *represent* them. In short, unlike the world of the dream, the mythico-religious world is believed to exist independently of the mental images and public symbols by which it is represented. In this sense, the images and symbols of the mythico-religious world are like the images of the dream-as-recalled, rather than those of the dream-as-dreamt. For when the dreamer awakens from his nocturnal slumber, he recognizes (in many societies at least) that the persons and events comprising his dream-as-dreamt had, in fact, consisted of his mental representations of them.

Nevertheless, the analogy between religion and the dream-as-dreamt still holds. In the latter, the images in the mind are not only reified, they are *externalized,* that is, these images of persons and events are not only taken for actual persons and events, but they are located in the external world, outside of the dreamer. In his waking life, however, the dreamer recognizes not only that the dream consists of images in his representational world, but that these images are representations of fantasied events, constructions of his mind, which occur not in the external, but in his internal world. In short, he recognizes that the dream is a hallucination.[1] The case of the religious believer, however, is rather different. Although distinguishing between the mythico-religious world, on the one hand, and the private images and public symbols by which it is represented, on the other, he nevertheless believes (in accordance with the teachings of his religious tradition) that these images and symbols signify real, rather than fantasied, beings and events which, as in the dream-as-dreamt, he locates in the external world.

Since, then, except for those who enter into trance and similar experiences, there is no experiential ground for believing in the external

---

[1] There are some primitive societies, of course, in which the dream-as-recalled is taken as a memory not of a nocturnal hallucination, but of an actual happening. For them, in short, the line between fantasy and reality (so far at least as dreams are concerned) is blurred. This does not mean that they are "pre-logical" in a wholesale sense, for the boundary between fantasy and reality is confined to a restricted domain. Nevertheless, it does mean that the primary process mode is a more prominent feature in the mental functioning of these societies than in those that do recognize the hallucinatory quality of the dream. It also means, moreover, that for such societies the reality of the mythico-religious world poses a problem of a much smaller magnitude than those in which the boundary between fantasy and reality is drawn much more sharply.

reality of the mythico-religious world, but the authority of tradition, the first problem posed by the analogy between religion and dreams is why the religious believer does not (like the awakened dreamer) awaken from his religious slumber and recognize that the mythico-religious world exists not in some external reality, but rather in the inner reality of the mind. The explanation, I think, is two-fold. First, there are obvious differences between the images and symbols of the mythico-religious world and those of the dream world. Second, there are certain characteristics of the mind which predispose human actors to believe in the external reality of the mythico-religious (but not of the dream) world.

Before examining the first explanation, something must be said about that slippery word, 'symbol,' which I have thus far been skirting. Following Charles Peirce, I use 'symbol' as one type of sign, a 'sign' being any object or event which represents and signifies some other object and event, or a class of objects and events. A symbol, then, is that type of sign in which (to shift from Peirce to Saussure) the relationship between the signifier and the signified is arbitrary. It is this dimension of the symbol which distinguishes it from Peirce's other two types of signs: the 'index,' in which there is a factual *contiguity* between signifier and signified, and the 'icon,' in which there is a factual *similarity* between them. By these definitions, a relic of the Buddha is (or is believed to be) an index of him; a sculpture of the Buddha is (or is believed to be) an icon of him; and the word "Buddha," is a symbol for him. Icons and symbols (but not indices) may be internal (i.e., we may have iconic or symbolic mental representations of objects or events) or they may be external (i.e., objects and events may be represented by physical icons and symbols in the external world). Cultural symbols and icons are, of course, external signs whose meanings are public (or shared) and conventional (handed down by tradition). With some few exceptions, of the kind already mentioned, cultural signs are symbols.

On the basis of this brief definitional excursus—I shall have more to say about icons and symbols below—we may now turn to the first difference between the dream world and the mythico-religious world which, as suggested above, might account for the belief in the external reality of the latter world, and its repudiation in the case of the dream world.

In reference to the dream world, it is necessary to distinguish between the dream-as-dreamt and the dream-as-recalled. (These two versions of the dream—in both versions I am concerned with the manifest content only—must also be distinguished, of course, from the dream-as-reported; but the latter version, important as it is for other purposes, is tangential to the purpose of this paper.) The dream-as-dreamt is a fantasy world which, represented in *private* and *internal* images (iconic and symbolic signs), is the dreamer's own creation. In constructing this world, the dreamer of course calls upon the memories of his own social experiences, the history of his group, cultural performances and traditions, and the like; but whatever its social and cultural inspirations, it is a representation of his own wishes and fears, hopes and anxieties. The dream-as-recalled is a representation, in memory (whether fragmentary or complete, distorted or veridical) of the dream-as-dreamt. Unlike the latter, however, which is experienced as an actual event, the dream-as-recalled is usually taken to be a memory of what the dream really is—a fantasied event. That it might, rather, be a memory of an actual event is usually contradicted by other events in the dreamer's waking life, as well as by the testimony of those of his fellows who may have comprised the *dramatis personae* of the dream.

Although the mythico-religious world is also a fantasy world, rather than invented by himself, it is *acquired* by the religious believer from his cultural traditions. These traditions, which proclaim the historicity and factuality of that world, are transmitted by means of cultural signs—the verbal symbols of religious doctrine and myth, and the visual symbols of ritual and sacred drama. Hence, unlike the dream world, the mythico-religious world is represented not only by the private and internal images of the religious believer, but also by the *public* and *external* symbols of his culture. Indeed, it is from these collective representations of the mythico-religious world that the dreamer constructs his mental representation of it.

In short, one possible explanation for religious believers holding to the external reality of the mythico-religious world, while denying such reality to the dream world, is that the latter is constructed from private thoughts, the former from cultural traditions. This difference has three important consequences. First, the reality of the mythico-religious world is not only *proclaimed* by the full authority of tradition, but it is *confirmed* by the ever-present (and psychologically compelling) cultural symbols from which the believer's representation of this world is constructed in the first place. Second, the fantasy quality which characterizes any mental representation consisting of images, is blunted in the case of the mythico-religious world because of its simultaneous representation in verbal symbols. Hence, unlike the dream-as-dreamt whose reality, upon awakening, is challenged by its chaotic, fragmentary, and often bizarre quality, the relatively systematic and coherent character of religious belief systems and myth narratives presents less of a challenge to the reality of the mythico-religious world. Third, since culturally-constituted symbols are public (and their meanings are therefore widely shared), the actor's belief in the correspondence between the mythico-religious world and his mental representation of it is confirmed by the consensual validation of his fellow.

Important as they are, these formal differences between the private images of the dream and the public symbols of religion are not, in my view, a sufficient explanation for the belief in the reality of the mythico-religious world. They do not explain, for example, why religious doctrines persist even in the face of competing, and often compelling, counter-claims of fact or reason, nor why cognitive dissonance is resolved not by abandoning the doctrines, but rather by resting their truth in faith. These facts (and others) suggest, as William James pointed out long ago, that religious belief ultimately rests on the actors' "will to believe," an intellectual posture which perhaps finds its extreme expression in Tertullian's precept *credo quia absurdum est*, I believe because it is absurd.

This brings us to the second explanation for the belief in the reality of the mythico-religious world mentioned above, for to speak of the will to believe is, of course, to shift our attention from the belief, and its representational medium, to the believer and his mind. In introducing this shift, I should like to distinguish "religion-as-a-doctrinal structure" from "religion-in-use," a distinction analogous to Saussure's distinction between 'langue' and 'parole.' By "religion-as-a-doctrinal structure" I refer to the organization of religious doctrines taken as a cognitive system, that is, a system of propositions together with their constituent meanings. In affirming these doctrines, the religious actor, unlike the religious philosopher, is concerned not only with their meanings, but also with what James termed their 'cash value.' That is, the religious actor is not so much interested in theory as in praxis (to employ a much over-worked distinction), and it is the latter dimension of religion to which I refer by the expression, "religion-in-use." As the expression indicates, this dimension refers to the purposes to which the religious actor puts his beliefs.

To say that religious actors are primarily concerned with religion-in-use is to say that although religious systems are cognitive systems, they persist not only because of the cognitive basis for the belief in the reality of the mythico-religious world, not even because its symbols are good to think, but because the belief in its reality satisfies some powerful human needs. In referring to the satisfaction of needs, I am of course alluding to the functions of religion—not, however, to its social functions, but to those which it serves for the religious actors themselves. Here I would follow Max Weber's contention that religion serves two universal functions, both of which are related to the vexatious problem of suffering—illness, death, drouth, loss, bereavement, madness, and so on. First, it provides answers to the intellectual problem of the *existence* of suffering and its seemingly unfair and inequitable distribution (the theodicy problem). Second, it provides various means for *overcoming* suffering, both as a temporary achievement and a permanent victory (salvation).

If, despite the remarkable cross-cultural diversity in its structure and content, religion universally serves (at least) these two functions, then it follows that the latter are related to two corresponding need-dispositions of the human mind which preadapt social actors to believe in the reality of their mythico-religious worlds. These comprise the need to explain and find 'meaning' in that which is otherwise inexplicable and meaningless, and the need to conquer the intolerable anxiety attendant upon painful and frightening situations that are beyond human ability to effect or control. If this proposition seems banal, it is never-

theless important to state as a reminder that even the most radical
cultural relativist can hardly begin to understand the persistence of
religion—or much else about human culture—without postulating
some set of need-dispositions as a universal characteristic of the
human mind.

Powerful as it might be, however, motivation alone is not a sufficient
explanation for the belief in the reality of the mythico-religious world.
Such a belief persists, I would suggest, because social actors are pre-
adapted cognitively, as well as motivationally, to believe in its reality.
Furthermore, I would suggest, this cognitive preadaptation is derived
from two biological (hence universal) characteristics of childhood—
prolonged helplessness and extended dependency—as a result of which
cultural systems, when viewed ontogenetically, are not the first resource
from which social actors construct their representational world.

Beginning from birth—hence prior to the acquisition of language
and the *culturally-constituted* conceptions of the world which language
makes possible—children develop what might be called *socially-constituted* conceptions as a consequence of (pre-linguistic) transactions
with parents and other parenting figures. Hence, long before they are
taught about the powerful beings who inhabit the mythico-religious
world young children have persistent and prolonged experiences, often
accompanied by intense affect, with these powerful beings who inhabit
their family world. Entirely helpless from birth, and absolutely dependent on these beings, young children form highly distorted, exagger-
ated, and even bizarre representations of these parenting figures. To
be sure, as they grow older most (but not all) children relinquish these
representations—often, however, after considerable struggle—in favor
of more realistic conceptions of them. At first, however, these bizarre
and distorted images, the products of primary process cognition, are
unconstrained by the secondary process cognition characteristic of
mature ego-functioning; that type of cognition which depends on the
achievement of 'object constancy,' language competence, and 'reality-
testing.' Let us examine each of these in turn.

Prior to the attainment of the developmental cognitive stage of
object constancy, the representations of different types of experience
with one and the same person are not yet integrated by the child so

as to form an organized, albeit differentiated, representation of him; rather, each type of experience produces a separate representation. Hence, although the actual parent is typically both good *and* bad, helpful *and* harmful, dependable *and* undependable, the young child, by a process known as 'splitting' forms separate images of a helping figure, a harming figure, a frustrating figure, and so on.

But even with the achievement of object constancy, it is difficult to form an integrated representation of one and the same person until the acquisition of language. For when images, rather than words, constitute the representational medium, the portrayal of different, but especially opposing, attributes of the same person—nurturant and punitive, good and bad, etc.—in a single image is difficult, if not impossible to achieve by means of such a medium, as any dreamer or sculptor knows. Hence, typically, the prelinguistic child forms different and opposing representations of the same parent, rather than one, conceptually integrated representation of him or her.

In addition to this cognitive basis, however, there is an equally important affective basis for the young child's splitting the opposing characteristics of his parents into separate representations. The integration of the loving and loved parent and the frustrating and hated parent into a single representation presupposes a degree of emotional maturity not yet attained by the young child. The inner conflict resulting from hating the person he loves, and is dependent upon, is beyond his emotional capacity to tolerate. Moreover, given the child's lack of reality testing, to hate someone is to destroy him, and since he both needs and loves the parent, this potentially intolerable conflict is obviated by splitting these opposing mental representations of the parent.

Having mentioned the concept of 'reality testing,' we may now explore its relevance for our thesis in greater detail. In order to do so, we shall once again return to the dream. I have already noted certain ways in which, with respect to their mental functioning, the cognitive *stage* of the prelinguistic child is similar in some respects to the cognitive *state* of the dreamer. I now wish to examine yet another similarity. The dream, I have already observed, is a nocturnal hallucination in which the dreamer, whose reality-testing is impaired, does not distinguish fantasy from reality, nor does he distinguish the fantasies themselves from the images by which they are represented, with the result that these images are reified.

Clinical data suggest that these same cognitive confusions may be found in the mental functioning of the prelinguistic child, not because his reality-testing is impaired, but because it is still undeveloped. Thus, for example, the young child's mental images of his parenting figures, just like dream images, may be reified, and thereby experienced as autonomous agents. Since, moreover, the boundary between inner and outer experience is blurred at this age, these reified agents may be experienced as located within himself (whence they are labeled, in the terminology of psychoanalysis, 'introjects'), or they may be externalized and located in the outer world (in which case they are labeled 'projections'). Although, as the ego develops, reifications are gradually given up they are nevertheless not reliquished easily, as is indicated by the projections which form the basis for the imaginary playmates of children, and by the introjects which are the basis for spirit possession. (Those few adults who never give up these reifications suffer severe psychopathology; for example, psychotic depression, in the case of persistent introjects, and paranoid delusions, in the case of persistent projections.) Rather than being relinquished, however, the externalized reifications of the early parental images may instead undergo a transformation, and it is this vicissitude of these projections with which we are concerned here.

In societies in which there is a high degree of integration between social and cultural systems, the child's early experiences with his parents may lead him to construct mental representations of them which, structurally, at least, are isomorphic with the mental representations of the superhuman beings of the mythico-religious world whose characteristics are only subsequently conveyed through the verbal and visual symbols of his culture. If one considers the typical mythico-religious world—with its gods and demons, saviors and satans, redeemers and destroyers—then it becomes apparent that the *socially-constituted* images which young children form of the powerful beings comprising their family world are highly similar to the *culturally-constituted* images which, at a later age, they form of the powerful beings comprising the mythico-religious world. Since, then, the former images, with all their bizarre distortions and exaggerations, represent and signify actual beings whose reality they have personally experienced, we may say that children are cognitively pre-adapted to believe in the reality of the superhuman beings that are represented and signified in the external collective representations of mythic narratives and religious ritual, as well as in the mental images which children form of them.

But given the fact that the child's early mental images of his parenting figures are reified and externalized, I would claim even more. For, I would suggest, when the child constructs his mental representations of the superhuman figures of the religious world, they may be merged (identified) with the corresponding representations he had previously constructed of the parenting figures of his family world, thereby forming a single representational world. When this occurs, the child's projections of his parental images may be retained without any psychopathological entailments, for they are then assimilated to his images of the superhuman beings whose existence is taught by religion and myth. At the same time, this process assures the belief in the external reality of these superhuman beings, for they are now merged with the reified and externalized images of those powerful human beings whose external reality he has himself experienced. (In rapidly changing societies, or in any other in which there is only minimal integration between social and cultural systems, the self-evident belief in the reality of the mythico-religious world is maximally jeopardized, with the result that the belief may be relinquished, or—as I have already observed— proclaimed as an article of faith.)

Thus, to take an example near home, when God is referred to as "Our Father who art in heaven," the cultural symbol, "Father," may be said to have two simultaneous meanings for the religious believer, one at the 'surface' level, the other at a 'deep' level. Since it is God who is designated as "Father," and since he is not literally conceived by the religious believer to *be* his father—whether genitor or pater— the surface meaning of "Father" is obviously a metaphorical one. That is, with respect to certain of his attributes—justice, mercy, love, etc.— God, who resides in heaven, is conceived to be *like* his father (pater) or, at any rate, like the normative conception of father, as that conception is informed by Western values regarding fatherhood. If, however, his mental representations of superhuman beings are merged with the religious believer's projections of his mental representation of the parents of childhood, then, in its deep meaning, "Father" is taken literally. For although God is not conceived by the believer to be his actual father (the one who is, or at least was, on earth), he is conceived, according to this explanation, as one of the reified and externalized representations of his childhood father—or a composite representation of some of them—which, in accordance with religious doctrine, the believer locates in heaven. Since in this sense, but in this sense only, God is indeed his father who is in heaven, in its deep meaning, "Father" is taken literally.

3

Let me summarize my argument thus far. My main point has been that the belief in the reality of the mythico-religious world, a belief in which culturally-constituted fantasy is invested with the appearance of reality, may be explained to a large extent as a function of the primary process mode of cognition. The cultural conceptions of the superhuman beings who inhabit that world are conveyed, of course, by the external cultural symbols by which they are represented—words, icons (sculpture and painting), and ritual—and from these collective representations the believer forms his mental representations of them. That these beings are believed to exist independently of the collective, as well as the mental, representations which signify them is best explained by the correspondence that exists between these representations and the mental representations that the young child previously forms of those actual powerful beings whose reality he has personally experienced—his parenting figures. These representations are based on the primary process mode of cognition because, in the absence of language, the representational medium consists of images; in the absence of object constancy, these images are formed by the process of splitting; and in the absence of reality testing, they are reified and externalized. It is the merging of the believer's mental representations of the mythico-religious beings with these projected mental representations of the parents of early childhood that constitutes the *cognitive* basis for the belief that the mythico-religious world exists independently of the collective representations by which it is both represented and signified.

By this explanation for the belief in the reality of the mythico-religious world, religious symbols have both 'surface' and 'deep' meanings, and no interpretation of any particular religion is complete unless its symbols are interpreted at both levels.[2] For this reason, the interpretation of religion (and other cultural systems) is similar to the interpretation of a dream in that the knowledge of its manifest content alone can be highly misleading without knowledge of its latent content.

According, then, to this explanation, the external and public symbols of religion—its collective representations—represent and signify at their 'surface' level the superhuman beings whose existence is affirmed by the various culturally parochial, religious traditions—Jahweh, Allah, Siva, the Madonna, Durga, and the like. These are their conscious and culturally variable meanings. At their 'deep' level, however, these symbols represent and signify the projections of the mental representations of the parents of early childhood. These are their unconscious, and culturally universal meanings. (Such an interpretation of the collective representations of religion might be contrasted with that of Durkheim who, it will be recalled, viewed them—in their 'deep' meanings—as signifying society.)

In sum, I have argued thus far, that underlying the cross-cultural diversity in the surface meanings of culturally parochial religious symbols, there are universal deep processes and meanings. If this is so, these cultural symbols effect three important psychological transmutations in the religious actors: transmutation of infantile into adult conceptions, of individual into public meanings, and of unconscious

---

[2] The current interest in cultural hermeneutics persistently distinguishes between interpretation and explanation, interpretation being viewed as a humanistic endeavor, concerned with intentions, purposes, goals, and the like, while explanation is viewed as a scientific or positivistic endeavor, concerned with the search for causal and functional 'laws.' In my view, this is a false dichotomy. If the former endeavor is concerned with producing valid, rather than just any kind of interpretations, it must be no less concerned with 'laws' than the former, because, of course, the cogency, if not validity of the idiographic interpretation is dependent on the nomothetic theory from which it is implicitly or explicitly deduced.

into conscious concerns. The satisfaction of these adult, public, and conscious concerns—especially those related to the explanation and conquest of suffering—constitutes, so I have argued, the most important manifest function of religion, providing a powerful motivational basis for the belief in the reality of the mythico-religious world.

However, if religious symbols also have deep meanings, then religion not only has manifest functions related to the surface meanings of these symbols, but it must also have latent functions related to their deep meanings. Hence in this, the concluding section of this paper, I wish to argue that religion attends not only to the conscious and public concerns of the actor's adult-like experience, but also to the unconscious and private concerns of his child-like experience. For if religious symbols are associated with unconscious infantile mental representations, it can only be because in addition to their conscious, adult concerns, social actors retain unconscious, infantile concerns, and it is their satisfaction that constitutes the latent function of religion. The intention of satisfying these concerns constitutes yet another—an unconscious—motivational basis for the belief in the reality of the mythico-religious world.

Since dreams constitute the most important private symbol system for the gratification, in fantasy, of infantile needs, I shall turn once again to the dream to help us understand the motivational aspects of unconscious symbolic processing. Since in this context, however, we are interested not in the hallucinatory, or ontological dimension of primary process cognition, but in its 'logical' dimension, we shall seek assistance from poetry as well. (The argument of this section of the paper is similar to, but also differs to some extent from one I have previously developed elsewhere. See Spiro 1977:xix–xxx.)

Should a poet wish to represent a conception of a friend—his bravery for example—he may convey this conception in a simple prose sentence, "John is brave"; in a figure of speech, such as the simile, "John is like a bull"; or in a trope, such as the metaphor, "John is a bull." In the metaphor, the intended meaning of the verbal symbol, "bull," is figurative rather than literal, for it is intended to represent the poet's conception of John, rather than to signify the brave bull in Madrid's corrida.

Unlike the poet, the dreamer has fewer degrees of freedom to express his thoughts because a representational medium consisting of images cannot directly represent qualities, such as bravery, which in language are represented by adjectives, adverbs, and similar parts of speech. In such a medium, which only contains the structural equivalents of nouns and verbs, the thought, "John is brave," cannot be represented in a form analogous to a simple sentence, let alone a simile. Rather, given the constraints of his medium, the dreamer, just like the painter or sculptor, can only represent such a thought in a form analogous to a trope. Hence, to represent the thought that John is brave, he may dream of a bull. Like the verbal trope of the poet, the visual trope of the dreamer can be misleading to one who does not understand the code. Thus, though the consciously intended meaning of the bull is figurative, rather than literal, inasmuch as an image of a bull is conventionally taken to be a representation of a certain species of bovine, it is a conventionally inappropriate sign for a human being. To put it in Peirce's classification of signs, although the image of the bull is intended as a *symbol* for John, its meaning will be misunderstood if it is taken as an *icon* for a bull. And this potential confusion is precisely one of the difficulties that is posed by the interpretation of dreams, as well as one of the reasons for their seemingly bizarre qualities. For although in the sleeping code by which he constructs his dream, the dreamer consciously intends the bull to be a symbolic representation of John, in his waking code by which he interprets the dream, it is taken by him to be an iconic representation of a bovine. In short, in the dream-as-recalled, the image of the bull is taken literally, though in the dream-as-dreamt it was intended figuratively.

The poet, of course, does not have an analogous problem—though his reader may—because he uses the same code in reading his poem that he had used when composing it. On both occasions, the conventionally inappropriate verbal symbol, "bull," is consciously understood by him to be a metaphor, a form which he chose in the first place in order to convey his conception of John more effectively, forcefully, or artistically than might have been achieved by a simple prose sentence. In short, both in the case of the poem and of the dream-as-dreamt, the figurative meaning of the sign—the word in the former, the image in the latter—is its consciously intended, and only, meaning.

In addition, however, to the representational constraints of his medium, the dreamer may set forth his thoughts in conventionally inappropriate images for yet another reason: the wish to disguise them. All of us have thoughts that are repugnant to our moral values, and since such thoughts are painful—they arouse moral anxiety—we often repress them, i.e., eliminate them from conscious awareness. Let us suppose, then, that in his waking state a dreamer has a repressed thought concerning his friend, John—the thought, for example, that he would like him to die. Let us further suppose that this thought continues in his sleep. If the dreamer were to distort this thought, by substituting a bull for John as the object of his wish, then he might, with moral impunity, gratify this disguised wish in a dream in which he kills a bull. In such a dream, the image of the bull has two meanings simultaneously—one literal, the other figurative. Its literal meaning (bull) is *consciously* intended, while its figurative meaning (John) is *unconsciously* intended. Since in this dream, unlike the first, the image is an unconscious symbol for John—consciously, of course, it is taken as an icon of a bull—the substitution of a bull for John is an example not of a trope, but of a defense mechanism; that is, it is a cognitive maneuver in which a forbidden wish undergoes unconscious symbolic distortion in the service of a disguise.

Let me now summarize very briefly the formal characteristics of defense mechanisms, in contrast to tropes, in somewhat more technical terms. (a) In a defense mechanism the symbolic distortion of the wish is *overdetermined,* that is, it is based on multiple and simultaneous motives, including the motives to gratify and—since it is forbidden—to disguise a wish. (b) Disguise and gratification alike are achieved by *displacement,* an unconscious process in which a conventionally inappropriate sign is substituted for an appropriate one. (Displacement is based on the same criteria—similarity or contiguity between the original and substituted objects signified by the two signs—that are employed in the symbolic substitutions found in metaphor, metonymy, synecdoche, and other tropes.) (c) Hence, the substitute sign is characterized by *condensation,* i.e., it has two or more simultaneously intended meanings, at least one of which is unconscious. (d) The conscious, or *manifest* meaning of the sign is its literal meaning; its unconscious, or *latent* meaning is its figurative meaning.

Let us now apply this analysis of the defensive use of the private symbols comprising the dream to the cultural symbols comprising religion. As a cultural system, religion attends in the first instance, as I have stressed more than once, to the public and conscious concerns of the believers' adult experience, especially their concern with suffering in both its intellectual and existential dimensions. That is, it attends to the needs to both explain and overcome suffering. To achieve the latter end, the religious actor engages in ritual transactions with the superhuman beings comprising the mythico-religious world. Some of these beings, kindly and benevolent, he turns to for assistance and aid in his attempt to cope with suffering. Others of them, aggressive and malevolent, are often viewed as the cause of suffering, and these he attempts to drive out or drive off. The former type arouse his wishes for and emotions of dependency and succorance; the latter type arouse his aggression, fear, and hatred.

Although such postures of dependency and aggression—whether expressed in the form of wishes, emotions, or actions—are culturally appropriate for adults in the religious contexts in which they are aroused and displayed, they are usually considered inappropriate for them in other contexts. There is one context, in particular, in which they are especially inappropriate; that context, of course, is the family. As the child's most significant others, his parents are at once his most important frustrating figures (consequently, the targets of his most intense aggressive feelings and wishes) and his most important nurturant figures (consequently the objects of his most intense dependency feelings and wishes). Parents are also, however, the very persons concerning whom, following an initial, culturally variable period of indulgence, the cultural prohibitions against dependency and aggression are most severe. The reasons are obvious. Social survival requires that children eventually outgrow their dependency on their family of origin, and that, having achieved independent status, they establish their own families and become objects for the dependency of their own children. Similarly, since aggression within the family is entirely disruptive of its integration, if not survival—hence inimical to its vital individual and social functions—it too must be prohibited.

This being so, every social actor and every society are confronted with an acute existential dilemma. Although his parents are the objects of the child's most intense dependency and aggressive needs and wishes, they are also the persons concerning whom their gratification is eventually most strongly frustrated. For although as children grow older and become adults, they learn to comply with the cultural norms prohibiting the overt display of aggression toward and dependency upon parents, this does not mean that these infantile needs are extinguished. That the contrary is the case is indicated not only by an abundance of clinical evidence, but also by commonplace observations of everyday life which indicate that these emotions and wishes are capable of arousal—and not only in a displaced form—in certain contexts, at least, and under certain provocations.

In sum, then, I am arguing that the intense dependency and aggressive wishes of children concerning parents, though seemingly extinguished, continue to exist in a repressed state in adults. Like all repressed wishes, these too seek gratification, and like them they are typically gratified—if they are gratified at all—in symbolic disguise. In addition to dreams, repressed wishes may be represented and (partially) gratified in the many privately constructed symbolic forms (including symptoms) which have been described and classified by psychiatrists. Typically, however, such wishes, particularly if they are widely shared, are represented and gratified in culturally-constituted rather than privately-constructed symbolic forms. Although many cultural systems—from games through politics—can be and have been used for this purpose, I would argue that religion is the system, *par excellence,* which is used for the disguised representation and gratification of the repressed wishes with which we are concerned here— dependency and aggressive wishes with regard to the parents of childhood. This is certainly the case in traditional societies, and if newspaper reports and television broadcasts can be taken as evidence, it is also the case, to a larger extent than we usually credit, in certain strata of modern society as well. That religion should be a focal system for the gratification of these wishes is hardly surprising if the explanation which I have offered for the meaning of its symbols is valid. For if the cultural symbols which represent the superhuman beings of the mythico-religious world signify, in their 'deep' meaning, the reified and externalized mental representations of the parents of childhood, what better way to express and gratify unconscious rage toward and dependency longings for these parents than through the vehicle of religious beliefs and rituals?

My thesis, then, is that when religious actors invoke the assistance of benevolent superhuman beings, or exorcise malevolent superhuman beings, they are not only *consciously* gratifying dependency and aggressive needs in regard to beings who are their *culturally appropriate* objects and targets, but they are also doing more than that. For if the actors' mental representations of these benevolent and malevolent superhuman beings are merged with the reified and projected representations of their kindly and hateful parents of childhood, then, they are simultaneously, but *unconsciously,* gratifying their dependency and aggressive needs in regard to their childhood parents, their *culturally inappropriate* objects and targets. That religion-in-use serves this (latent) function explains at least one of the unconscious motivational bases for the belief in the reality of the mythico-religious world. I might add that if this argument is valid, religion also serves an equally important latent function for society. For if religion-in-use is a means for the symbolic gratification of these powerful infantile needs, society is thereby spared the highly disruptive consequences of their direct gratification. But that is a topic for another paper.

*   *   *

We may now summarize the implications of this paper, with respect to both its specifically religious argument and its more general cultural-symbolic argument. The former argument has been concerned with only one problem related to the explanation of religious systems, the problem of why religious actors believe in the reality of the mythico-religious world. Whether or not the particular solution offered here is correct is less important, however, than its underlying thesis that a comprehensive explanation for such a belief must attend to at least three dimensions of the problem: (a) the private, as well as public meanings of religious symbols; (b) their 'deep,' or socially acquired meanings, as well as their 'surface,' or culturally transmitted meanings; and (c) the latent, as well as the manifest functions of the actor's belief that these symbols signify a real, and not merely a representational

world. An explanation that ignores any of these dimensions is, I have
tried to show, incomplete.

To arrive at such a comprehensive explanation, I further attempted
to show, we must be as much concerned with the properties and
processes of the human mind as with the properties of cultural symbols
and the doctrines which they represent. Although Durkheim's insistence
that collective representations constitute the focus of anthropological
investigation marked a giant leap forward in the study of socio-cultural
systems, he made a serious error in ruling out the study of mental
representations as irrelevant to their study. For, as this paper has
attempted to show, any cultural system is a vital force in society so
long as there is a correspondence between the symbols in which cultural
doctrines are represented and their representation as beliefs in the minds
of social actors. When such a correspondence does not obtain, a cultural
system may yet survive, but it survives as a fossil—as a set of clichés—
rather than as a living force. If this is so, then the study of mental
representations is no less important than that of collective representations for the anthropological enterprise.

My argument makes an even more radical claim, namely, that in
attending to the human mind it is as important to understand its
unconscious, as well as its conscious processes. Although a knowledge
of conscious cognitions and motives can help us to understand the
'surface' meanings and manifest functions of cultural symbols, knowledge of unconscious cognitions and motives is required to understand
their 'deep' meanings and latent functions. Lest I be misunderstood,
I have not argued, as an older generation of psychoanalytic theorists
was sometimes prone to do, that the latter meanings and functions are
more important for the understanding of symbols (whether cultural or
non-cultural) than the former. I have argued, however, that they are no
less important.

ACKNOWLEDGEMENTS

I am indebted to Jacques Maquet and Walter Goldschmidt for inviting me to participate in the second series of lectures in honor of Harry Hoijer, and to Roy G. D'Andrade, Fitz John Poole, Theodore Schwartz, Marc J. Swartz, and Donald F. Tuzin for their valuable criticisms of an earlier draft of this paper. I wish to acknowledge my gratitude to the National Institute of Mental Health for its support of a research project on the comparative study of culturally-constituted defense mechanisms, some of whose findings are incorporated in this paper.

REFERENCES

Spiro, Melford E.
    1969   Discussion. In *Forms of Symbolic Action,* ed. by Robert F. Spencer. Seattle: University of Washington Press (for the American Ethnological Society), pp. 208–214.

    1977   *Kinship and Marriage in Burma.* Berkeley: University of California Press.

    1978   *Burmese Supernaturalism.* Expanded edition. Philadelphia: Institute for the Study of Human Issues.

EMBLEMS OF IDENTITY:
A SEMIOTIC EXPLORATION

Milton Singer

The subtitle of the present paper, "A Semiotic Exploration," refers to Charles Peirce's definition of semiotic as a general theory of signs. The relevance of his semiotic for an analysis of emblems will be found in his definition of sign as a triadic relation of sign, object, and interpretant; his distinction between iconic or mimetic, indexical or deictic, and symbolic signs; his conception of the self as a semiotic system that is formed in a matrix of social relations; and his generally phenomenological and pragmatic approach to questions of epistemology and ontology. The implications of Peirce's semiotic for a semiotic anthropology in general, and for a semiotics of emblems in particular, remain to be fully developed (Singer 1978, 1980; Sebeok 1975:248–9).

Although several specific studies of special emblematic signs have been made (see Waddington 1974, Upensky 1976, and Firth 1973), and some useful suggestions have been advanced by Jakobson (1971) in his discussion of the distinction between visual and auditory signs, by Lyons (1977) on "secondary iconization," by Wallis (1975) on "semantic enclaves," and by Eco (1976) on "stylization," the application of Peirce's general theory of signs to the formulation of a semiotics of emblems has hardly begun.

Peirce, himself, did not analyze emblems of identity semiotically.[1] However, he did mention a *standard* or *ensign,* a *badge,* and a *church creed* as examples of "symbols" in ancient Greek usage in order to justify his proposed definition of "symbol" as a conventional sign (Buchler 1955:113–14). While a "symbol" is for Peirce a *kind* of thing and denotes a *kind* of thing and therefore a law or regularity of the indefinite future, "a law necessarily governs or 'is embodied' in individuals, and prescribes some of their qualities" (ibid., p. 112). Consequently, both an icon, which signifies a quality and an index, which denotes an individual may be constituents of a symbol. A symbol without an associated icon and index would not exhibit the qualities signified or identify the objects denoted (ibid., p. 114). It is in this particular respect that Peirce's semiotic is especially suited for an analysis of emblems such as banners and badges, concrete sign complexes that combine symbols, icons, and indices. A national flag, for example, as a product of national agreement, is a "symbol," but also includes iconic features in its insignia (such as stars, a cross, a crescent, or a hammer and sickle) and indexical features in its unique combination of color bars and insignia. Any particular national flag can be analyzed as a member of a *system* of symbols in which the permutations and affiliations of elements can be specified and traced synchronically and historically (*cf.* Firth 1973:Chap. 10). The suggestion, extrapolated from Peirce, that emblems are conventional signs, or "symbols" by his definition, does not exclude iconic and indexical signs from emblems. On the contrary, the conventional feature of an emblem may consist of an agreement to include certain "natural signs" such as iconic insignia and indexical identifiers (*cf.* Silverstein 1976:27).

Within the context of the national flags example it is also useful to distinguish between the *manifest* and the *latent* identities of an emblem. The manifest identity is signified or shown by the iconic signs of the emblem, say a crescent moon or a star in a national flag. The

---

[1] Max Fisch, the general editor of the new edition of Peirce's papers, has found no record as yet in his complete collection of Peirce manuscripts of any mention of the term "emblem" by Peirce. He did find in Peirce's interleaved copy of *The Century Dictionary* the following entry: "emblemist, n. Quarles the *Emblemist,* Southey, Doctor xlviii." Fisch interprets this to mean that Peirce noticed the omission of "emblemist" and supplied a reference (Fisch to Singer 8 Aug. 1980, see Gilman 1980).

latent identity of an emblem, however, is not restricted to any of the familiar celestial objects signified by the insignia but also includes the association of people whose badge of membership is a particular kind of flag and insignia. The manifest identity of an emblem is usually quite transparent from the iconic features of the emblem, the qualities they exhibit, and objects they denote. The latent identity is not usually transparently visible, except to those already familiar with the emblem and its conventional meaning. Strangers need to infer the latent identity from attached proper names, verbal legends, and similar explanations. The latent identies of the elephant and the donkey as symbols of the Republican and the Democratic parties respectively, for example, are quite familiar to most Americans; to foreigners, however, only the manifest identities of these symbols would be obvious while their latent identities as political badges would need to be learned.

One major thesis of Durkheim's emblem theory of totemism can be reformulated and clarified in terms of the relationship between the manifest and latent identities of totemic emblems. The plants, animals, and other natural phenomena represented by totemic emblems are the manifest identities of these emblems; the clan, the moiety, the groups of men or of women, the individual whose badge the totemic emblem becomes, are the latent identities of the emblem (*cf.* Nadel 1964:261, 1965:263. See Umiker-Sebeok and Sebeok 1976:Introduction for the semiotics of aboriginal sign languages.) Levi-Strauss's interpretation of totemism in terms of homologies between two systems of differences, natural and cultural, is an assertion that the differences between the manifest identities of the emblems form a system which is homologous to the system of diffferences between the latent identities, social groups, and individuals. He affirms such homologies as a "postulate"; whether they can also be empirically demonstrated will be critically discussed.

How the nonverbal features of an emblem, especially its iconic signs, make a statement of identity is explained by Peirce in his discussion of the object of an icon:

> The object of an Icon is entirely indefinite, equivalent to "something." . . . A pure picture without a legend only says "something is like this." . . . To attach a legend to the

picture makes a sentence . . . analogous to a portrait we
will say of Leopardi with Leopardi written below it. It con-
veys its information to a person who knows who Leopardi
was, and to anybody else it only says something called
Leopardi looked like this. [*CP* 8:183.][2]

The use of an emblem to make a statement of identity need not
involve a verbal legend or other verbal expression since the iconic and
indexical signs in the emblem, as well as previous acquaintance with
the objects of the emblem and with the conventional usages, may be
sufficient to make an identity statement. The wearing of religious,
political, or fraternal insignia, for example, often serves to make statements of identity, although when there is doubt or dispute concerning
the interpretation of the emblems, verbal explanations are quickly
introduced.

The electrician in Ohio, for example, who explained his and some
of his colleagues' refusal during the Iranian hostage crisis to remove
American flag decals from their hard hats, even under threat of being
fired, expressed a popular and widespread belief that the display of
certain kinds of emblems "says something" and makes a statement of
identity. The electricians, by placing the flag on their hard hats, were
saying that they were patriotic Americans who supported the hostages
in Iran. Because their verbal explanations are available, the interpretation of the "message" can be verified:

> In America, hats are the sign of individuality. The hat says
> who you are. . . . Hard hats and the flag go together like
> motherhood and apple pie; they're one and the same. [*Chi-
> cago Tribune*, 17 March 1980.]

Peirce emphasizes, in the Leopardi and in many other examples,
the necessity for a previous or "collateral" acquaintance with the object
of the sign. "No sign," he explains, "can be understood—or at least
. . . no *proposition* can be understood—unless the interpreter has

[2] References to Peirce's *Collected Papers* will be indicated, as is usual, by volume
and paragraph. *CP* 8:183 should be read as *Collected Papers* Volume 8, paragraph
183.

'collateral acquaintance' with every object of it" (*CP* 8:183). This perspective suggests the importance of anthropological fieldwork and monographs for understanding emblems of identity. A purely formal or structural analysis of emblems must be supplemented by a contextual study if we are to become acquainted with the objects the emblems denote and the identities to which they refer.

Iconic signs in emblems represent their objects by some mode of similarity or analogy. In Peirce's semiotic there may be three kinds: *images*, or pictures which represent their objects through a resemblance in qualities; *diagrams*, which represent the relations between the parts of their objects by analogous relations in their own parts (i.e., as homologies); and *metaphors*, which represent a parallelism in their objects with themselves. While iconic signs may occur naturally, they are often the products of human construction. For example, "the design an artist draws of a statue, pictorial composition, architectural elevation, or piece of decoration" is an iconic sign by the contemplation of which the artist "can ascertain whether what he proposes will be beautiful and satisfactory" (Buchler 1955:106). Similarly, Peirce suggests, mathematicians construct geometrical diagrams and algebraic arrays as iconic signs by the observation of which they can discover new truths (ibid., pp. 106–7, 135–49).

Iconic signs do not of themselves assert anything; they signify a character. Taken together with indexical and symbolic signs, however, they become predicates of propositional statements, as Peirce explains with the example of Leopardi's portrait and the legend. Since (preabstract) paintings and diagrams depend on conventional rules for their interpretation, according to Peirce, they include indexical and symbolic as well as iconic signs. It is for this reason that Jakobson speaks of "symbolic icons" (1971:129).

A semiotic analysis of emblems as constructed signs, thus, requires an understanding of the characters they signify, of the objects they denote, and of the system of conventional signs ("symbols") they use to make statements about the relations among emblems, objects, and characters. Such understandings will be realized in the dialogues between the designers of the emblems (the "utterers") and the viewers (the "interpreters") in the context of ongoing social interactions.

The study of emblems as multimedia symbolic representations in the context of cultural performances also provides a semiotic approach to the study of art and ritual forms as cultural systems (see Geertz 1973, 1976; Turner 1967; Redfield 1962; and Wolf 1958). The cultural performance concept emerged in my Madras studies when I found that "the social organization of tradition," in Robert Redfield's words, included a wide variety of religious and secular performances in which people exhibited their culture. When I applied the concept to study American identity, Lloyd Warner's "Yankee City" monograph, *The Living and the Dead* (1959), suggested a valuable base-line and the important "emblem" concept both as a Durkheimian collective representation and as a "condensed" (in the sense of Freud 1938 and Sapir 1934) and primarily visual symbol of the culture (Warner 1959:449–50, 474–6). By emphasizing constructed emblems of identity I hope to make explicit what is largely implicit in Durkheim and Warner: that the natural objects denoted by emblems are the manifest objects of the emblems, and that there are utterers and interpreters of an emblem who denote, through its use, a particular social group with which they identify or from which they separate themselves. In this respect, the use of an emblem implies an assertion or denial of membership in a particular social group.

It is encouraging to see that the increase in space-flights is leading to an increasing use of images of the planet earth as an emblem of humanity. These images are becoming for some people magic cosmic diagrams, *mandalas* and *yantras,* through which to assert one's membership in the human species.

These preliminary remarks explain why a semiotic exploration of emblems of identity looks for such emblems in anthropological studies of Australian totemism and in Yankee City Memorial Day ceremonies and Tercentenary celebrations.

1

When our revisits to "Yankee City" first began in 1974, we were attracted to a well-organized annual nine-day celebration of "Yankee Homecoming." This usually included a great variety of community events such as flea markets and fashion shows, arts and crafts fairs, concerts, lunches and suppers, road races and dances, house tours and historical presentations, family and high school reunions. While first introduced in 1957 as a commercial promotion, the "Homecomings" have become a set of genuine community-wide affairs, enlisting the cooperation of many local organizations and volunteers. The celebrations which begin at the end of July have even come to replace July Fourth celebrations culminating with the "Jimmy Fund" Parade. With marching bands and colorful floats, it draws crowds of spectators, many returning "home" from newer residences, who line High Street from an early hour. Along with Bicentennial reenactments and other special events added in 1975 and 1976, the "Yankee Homecomings" constitute cultural performances in which the citizens of Yankee City not only engage in summer fun and games, but also "collectively state what they believe themselves to be." The phrase quoted was used by Warner (1959) to characterize the major theme of the five days in July 1930 devoted to historical processions, parades, games, religious ceremonies, sermons, and speeches in celebration of the Tercentenary of the Massachusetts Bay Colony:

> At that moment in their long history, the people of Yankee City as a collectivity asked and answered these questions: Who are we? How do we feel about ourselves? Why are we what we are? Through the symbols publicly displayed at this time when near and distant kin collected, the city told its story. [Warner 1959:107.]

In another paper, I have compared the 1930 Tercentenary to the 1970 Yankee Homecoming and Bicentennial as cultural performances, and have also discussed the meaning of the persistent local interest in historical authenticity (see Singer 1977). In the present paper I should like to approach some of these questions from the point of view of the

special symbols and symbolic representations, which Warner called
"emblems," that symbolize collective and individual identities in the
city. In addition to the "Yankee Homecomings" and Bicentennial
activities which we observed and studied in the summers of 1974,
1975, and 1976, observations and interviews concerning an urban
renewal and restoration project made during these and later years,
interviews of selected families in 1977, and archival research in 1978
are also drawn upon. (Separate papers concerning the 1977 and 1978
observations, interviews, and research are in preparation.)

The Concise Oxford Dictionary of Current English (1976) lists two
major meanings for "emblem": 1) symbol, typical representation of
a person or a quality, and 2) heraldic device or symbolic object as a
distinctive badge. The American College Dictionary (1959) gives a
more expanded version of the first meaning for "emblem": symbol—
an object, or a representation of it, symbolizing a quality, state, class
of persons, etc. The second listed meaning, instead of heraldic device,
is "an allegorical drawing or picture, often with explanatory writing."
Both dictionaries give "emblematize" as a verb: to serve as an emblem,
to represent by an emblem. Emblems as allegorical pictures or diagrams
with some written didactic motto were well known in the Renaissance
through "emblem books" (Praz 1964). These, however, are only
indirectly connected with the emblems of identity which are the subject
of this paper. The carving of allegorical drawings and mottos on gravestones which are otherwise identified by name and town and city seals,
connect the two kinds of emblems. Ancient Mesopotamian emblems,
or "divine symbols" as Oppenheim calls them—designs of the sun
disc, chariot of the sun, the eight-pointed star of Ishtar, crescent, dog,
lion, snake, eagle, and heraldic symbols—were inscribed on oval
stones used as boundary markers (kudurru's) in the fields to proclaim
and protect royal grants, from 1380 B.C. to 648 B.C. According to
Oppenheim, these symbols corresponded to the major deities of the
pantheon, were provided with partially identifying inscriptions, and
were objects of worship in which the presence of a specific deity was
recognized (Oppenheim 1964:286–7).

Warner, and other anthropologists who have used the term "emblem,"
have undoubtedly been acquainted with the dictionary definitions and

popular usages of the term (Wagner 1978:7, 26; Musée Guimet 1964; Tarn 1976). These have not, however, been the chief source of anthropological interest or usage. That derives from the association of emblems with totemism in Australia and North America. The first serious and systematic development of an emblem theory of totemism was probably Durkheim's in his *Elementary Forms of the Religious Life,* first published in France in 1912. "The totem is a name first of all, and then, . . . an emblem" (Durkheim 1947:110).

Durkheim himself notes that the analogy of totems with flags and heraldic devices has often been made; he frequently quotes his ethnographic sources, Spencer and Gillen, and Schoolcraft among others, on the analogy (see Schoolcraft 1851, I:420). He states the heraldic analogy quite explicity:

> The nobles of the feudal period carved, engraved and designed in every way their coats-of-arms upon the walls of their castles, their arms, and every sort of object that belonged to them; the blacks of Australia and the Indians of North America do the same thing with their totems. [Durkheim 1947:113–14.]

His ethnographic examples from both North America and Australia include painted totemic emblems on shields, ensigns, helmets, clan totemic designs first on ornaments, paintings, and tents, and then on door posts, walls, and woodwork of houses when society became sedentary. Canoes, utensils, funeral piles, the grounds and trees near tombs, and coffin-like hollowed wood are engraved with totemic designs. Also, a very general custom in religious ceremonies and rites of initiation and funerals was painting bodies with totemic designs (ibid., pp. 114–19).

Closely related to the painting or tattooing of totemic emblems on the body are the practices which imitate the totem in some respect (hair style, cosmetics, garments, bodily movements). "It is a very general rule," Durkheim writes, "that the members of each clan seek to give themselves the external aspect of their totem" (1947:116). Among the Omaha, for example, members of the turtle clan wear their

hair shaved off except for six bunches, two on each side of the head,
one in front and one behind, to imitate the legs, head and tail of a
turtle.

Durkheim also stated the analogy between totem and flag quite
explicitly and used it to illustrate and, perhaps, guide his own analysis
of the symbolic nature of the totem and its psychological effects. The
flag was for him the paradigmatic example of a simple, definite, and
easily representable symbol whose emotional effects depend on a
"transference of sentiments" aroused by what the flag symbolizes:

> The soldier who dies for his flag, dies for his country; but
> as a matter of fact, in his own consciousness, it is the flag
> that has the first place. . . . He loses sight of the fact that
> the flag is only a sign, and that it has no value in itself, but
> only brings to mind the reality that it represents; it is treated
> as if it were this reality itself. . . . Now the totem is the
> flag of the clan. . . . [Durkheim 1947:220.]

Durkheim's theory has been both greatly criticized and developed
since it was first published. Even though W.E.H. Stanner called Durkheim's theory "a brilliant muddle," he thinks highly enough of the
contribution to want to preserve it from that oblivion to which he would
consign all other early works on totemism (Stanner 1965:236). In fact,
his own analysis of the "totemic sign-function" is itself an indirect
testimonial to Durkheim's early insight into Australian totemism as a
part of a "vast social symbolism" and his conception of it as a "language" (Durkheim 1947:126–127:4, 231; Stanner 1965:228, 232).
Nancy Munn's brilliant, recent study of Walbiri graphic signs as a
semiotic system is also a kind of fulfillment, if not a complete veri-
fication, of Durkheim's theory of totemic emblems (Munn 1973:77,
177, 216, 217; Durkheim 1947: 126–7, 230–4; Yengoyan 1980).

According to Raymond Firth's assessment, Durkheim "focused
our attention upon the significance of a symbol for the corporate character of human conceptualization and sentiment" (Firth 1973:134).

When the object chosen as symbol was of human design—and for
Durkhem it was usually so—it was a totemic *emblem,* painted, engraved
or carved images among the Indians of North America, and essentially

of geometric design among the Australians (Durkheim 1947:126–7). Even when the object chosen as symbol was identified in nature—a species of plant, animal, or natural phenomenon—that object remains the object of a symbol, either as the member of a natural species symbolizing its own kind or as a totemic *emblem:*

> It is the figurative representation of this plant or animal and the totemic emblems and symbols of every sort, which have the greatest sanctity . . . thus the totem is before all a symbol, a material expression, of something else. [Durkheim 1947:206, 216.]

The totemic animals represented by the emblems "become sacred because they resemble the totemic emblem," more so, perhaps, than human beings resemble the totemic emblems. This, for Durkheim, explains why the totemic animals are treated as elder brothers (Durkheim 1947:133, 139, 222). Surrounded by the signs of their totems, natural or constructed, the Australians found in their totemic emblems "the permanent element of social life" which endured "after the assembly has been dissolved" and with the changing generations (Durkheim 1947:221; *cf.* Stanner 1965:227–8, 236–7; Munn 1973:215).

I do not wish to claim too much for Durkeim's theory of totemism. It may be enough to recognize that his was one of the first theories to show how totemic names and emblems were related to ritual and myth, to religious beliefs and sentiments, to language and the logic of classification, to cosmology, morality, and history, to social organization, as well as to the performing and practical arts. Whatever has been the fate of specific elements of Durkheim's emblem theory, it is a remarkable tribute to find the major terms of discussion and debate still couched in largely Durkheimian language and concepts.

2

It is interesting that both Radcliffe-Brown and Levi-Strauss rejected the primary importance Durkeim assigned to the emblem analogy. Recognizing with Durkheim that "the sentiments of attachment to a group shall be expressed in a formalized collective behavior having reference to an object that represents the group itself," Radcliffe-Brown nevertheless explained the choice of such objects, whether a flag, a king, a president, or a totemic emblem, in a manner very different from Durkheim (Radcliffe-Brown 1952:124–5). Radcliffe-Brown rejected Durkheim's explanation for the selection of natural species of plants and animals as emblems or representatives of clans and other social groups on the grounds that in Australia, at least, no totemic emblems could be found for either sex totemism, moiety totemism, section totemism, or even for clan totemism among many tribes. Radcliffe-Brown argued that where totemic designs were found, in Central and Northern Australia, the natural species was sacred because they were "already objects of the ritual attitude . . . by virtue of the general law of the ritual expression," and not because they had been selected as representatives of social groups, or emblems, as Durkheim maintained. The general law to which Radcliffe-Brown refers, first stated in his study of the Andaman Islanders, asserts that:

> Any object or event which has important effects upon the well-being (material or spiritual) of a society, or any thing which stands for or represents any such object or event, tends to become an object of the ritual attitude. [Radcliffe-Brown 1952:129.]

Thus, according to Radcliffe-Brown's explanation, any emblem or design which stands for or represents such a natural species will also tend to become sacred or an object of the ritual attitude.

Levi-Strauss has called this generalized explanation for the selection of totemic species found in Radcliffe-Brown's first paper on totemism (1929), a form of naturalism, empiricism, and functionalism, and contrasts it unfavorably with the explanation in Radcliffe-Brown's second paper on totemism (1952). In the second paper, Levi-Strauss finds a structuralist analysis very similar to his own:

> The animals in totemism cease to be solely or principally creatures which are feared, admired, or envied: their perceptible reality permits the embodiment of ideas and relations conceived by speculative thought on the basis of empirical observations. We can understand, too, that natural species are chosen not because they are "good to eat" but because they are "good to think." [Levi-Strauss 1963:89.]

The formulation that so impressed Levi-Strauss concerned the principle by which specific pairs of birds were selected to represent the moieties of a dual division. Levi-Strauss suggests that "instead of asking 'why all these birds?' we can ask why particularly eagle hawk and crow, and other pairs?" (ibid., p. 86). Radcliffe-Brown's answer, that in all cases of exogamous moieties the particular pairs of birds chosen to represent them (such as eagle hawk and crow) were chosen because they are in a relation of "opposition"—in a double sense— as "friendly antagonists" and as "contraries by reason of their character," was for Levi-Strauss genuinely structuralist. It attempted to relate institutions, representations, and situations through their respective relations of opposition and correlation, and in conformity with every anthropological undertaking, it asserted "a homology of structure between human thought in action and the human object to which it is applied" (Levi-Strauss 1963:90, 91).

For Levi-Strauss, Radcliffe-Brown's second paper is an example of his own conception of totemism as a coordination of two systems of differences: a natural series of animal and plant species, and a cultural series of human social units; this is a new conception deriving from structural linguistics and structural anthropology, and represents a departure from Radcliffe-Brown's earlier naturalism, empiricism, and functionalism (ibid., p. 90). Regardless of criticisms of both his own theories and his interpretation of Radcliffe-Brown's formulations (see Fortes 1966), and though he frequently refers to the "totemic illusion" and to "so-called-totemism," Levi-Strauss's analysis constitutes a contribution to a positive theory of totemism. (Hiatt 1966, for one, has pointed this out.)

In all probability there was a growing emphasis in Radcliffe-Brown's later papers (during the 1940s) on relational and structural analysis of social structure and kinship systems, joking and avoidance relations, and totemism. (This emphasis most likely derived from his interest in Russell's and Whitehead's philosophy of science based on events and relational structures rather than from structural linguistics or structural anthropology. See Singer 1973.) But in turning toward a relational and structural analysis of both the natural and cultural systems and beginning to de-emphasize naturalistic and functionalistic explanations, he did not reinstate Durkheim's emblem theory or develop an alternative symbolic analysis. Curiously, in his second paper he formulates one of the general problems of totemism in Durkheimian terms but then sets it aside without further explanation. In question is

> the problem of how social groups come to be identified by connection with some emblem, symbol, or object having symbolic or emblematic reference. A nation identified by its coat of arms, a particular congregation of a church identified by its relation to a particular saint, a clan identified by its relation to a totemic species; these are all so many examples of a single class of phenomena for which we have to look for a general theory. [Radcliffe-Brown 1958:113–14.]

Radcliffe-Brown's failure to develop a general theory of how particular social groups or individuals came to be identified by particular emblems may be explained by his desire to avoid particularistic historical studies and his emphasis on totems as natural objects rather than constructed emblems. However, a more important reason, I believe, is precisely his development of a structuralist analysis in his second paper; structuralist analysis tends to abstract from individuals and individual collections of individuals. To deal with the individual objects of iconic signs, it is necessary, as Peirce pointed out, to have previous acquaintance with them and to employ indexical signs such as personal pronouns, demonstrative and relative pronouns, and "selectives" such as "any" and "some" for finding the objects (*CP* 8:181).

The problem is highlighted by Levi-Strauss who on the one hand postulated an homology between two systems of differences, one of which occurs in nature and the other in culture, yet on the other hand asserts that:

> This structure would be fundamentally impaired if homologies between the terms themselves were added to those between their relations or if, going one step further, the entire system of homologies were transferred from relations to terms. . . . In this case the implicit content of the structure would no longer be that clan 1 differs from clan 2 as for instance the eagle differs from the bear but rather that clan 1 is like the eagle and clan 2 is like the bear. [Levi-Strauss 1966:115.]

The theoretical implications of such a transformation in the homologies are for Levi-Strauss momentous:

> When nature and culture are thought of as two systems of differences between which there is a formal analogy, it is the systematic character of each domain which is brought to the fore. . . . But if social groups are considered not so much from the point of view of their reciprocal relations in social life as each on their own account, in relation to something other than social reality, then the idea of diversity is likely to prevail over that of unity. [1966:116.]

The difficulty posed by this postulate is not only an ethnographic one—whether such transformations and homologies in fact occur. Levi-Strauss (1966) himself has documented some examples of the decay of totemic systems, and Dumont (1970) has applied the analysis to the "substantialization" of castes in India and to racism in the West. (See also Levi-Strauss 1963; Schwartz 1975; Boon and Schneider 1974; and Boon 1979.) The difficulty is, rather, a theoretical one, analogous to that encountered by Radcliffe-Brown: how social groups come to be identified by connection with some emblem, symbol, or object having symbolic or emblematic reference, if there are only formal relations between the social groups and they are not involved separately. Since Levi-Strauss rejects both Pierce's indexical signs and Russell's demonstrative pronouns as symbolic devices for identifying individuals and social groups, it is not clear how he bridges the gap between his postulated structural homologies and the denotation of some *particular* social groups presupposed by the structural comparisons (Levi-Strauss 1966:214–16). It is not enough to compare clan 1 and clan 2 as being contraries and friendly antagonists like Eaglehawk and Crow; it is necessary, in addition, to use indexical signs, proper names or other devices to denote the particular social groups whose relationships are being compared with the relations between Eaglehawk and Crow. Such indexical signs identify the terms related but do not necessarily replace the relations by terms.

Stanner has tried to integrate the apparently disparate aspects of totemism—structural, symbolic, and substantive—by interpreting a collective totemic emblem as "an abstract symbol for the possible membership, over all space and time, of the sets of people symbolized by it —the dead, the living, the unborn. . . . Any particular instance of a totem at a place or point of time is, in the symbolic sense, an image of the whole indefinite family of sets." He reports that a thoughtful Aboriginal once said to him "There are Honey People all over the world" (Stanner 1965:229). But this interpretation stresses the structural and symbolic aspects of the concept, leaving the denotative aspects problematic: "not *this* eaglehawk or *that* crow, but all and any eaglehawks or crows that were, are, or might be" (Stanner 1965:228). Also, his explanation of a collective totem as an abstract symbol omits to note the singularity of the totemic sign. Peirce's conception of an emblematic sign's *objective generality* offers a solution to the problem:

> A statue of a soldier on some village monument, in his overcoat with his musket, is for each of a hundred families the image of its uncle, its sacrifice to the Union. That statue then, though it is itself single, represents any one man of whom a certain predicate may be true. It is *objectively* general. [Buchler 1955:263; see also *CP*8:357.]

In Stanner's interpretaion of totems as abstract symbols, the predicates are iconic signs, or, as he describes "the totemic idiom . . . an imagery mimetic of vital or significant things in the environment" (1965:236). That imagery may seem exotic to Westerners but,

> the fact that hunters and foragers developed a zoomorphic and phytomorphic imagery was as appropriate to men in the Australian environment as that nomadic shepherds developed a pastoral imagery in the environment of early Judea and Israel. [Stanner 1965:237.]

The problem for Stanner is not the particular kind of imagery, rather, it is Durkheim's problem of "how the associating of a totem with a collection of people was that which transformed them from just a collection into groups with a sign of unity" (Stanner 1965:237).

In dealing with this problem Stanner gives more importance to history and the "irreducibly arbitrary" nature of the associations between totems and particular places and groups of people which have some features in common (ibid., p. 226). At the same time he emphasizes, more than Durkheim, that the totemic system symbolizes a link between cosmogony, cosmology, and ontology; as well as symbolizing aboriginal totemic groups as perennial corporations of a religious character.

The movement for critical revision of Durkheim's emblem theory of totemism that began with Radcliffe-Brown's 1929 "sociological theory" of totemism and culminated in 1962 (1966) with Levi-Strauss's "postulate" of homology between two systems of differences, natural and cultural, has raised new questions. One such question is whether the plants, animals, and natural objects selected as totems actually constitute "systems" of totemic symbols or are unsystematic and *ad hoc*.

Hiatt, critical of Levi-Strauss's homology hypothesis as well as his attempt to explain away unsystematic totemism (by appealing to historical and demographic changes that may have dismantled previously existing totemic systems), believes that "the choice of totemic symbols has always proceeded unsystematically." He urges a return to Durkheim's "assumption that, in general, group symbols signify both unity and difference, and are vitalized by affectivity" (Hiatt 1965:90). This perspective leaves the field open for a realistic and pluralist position, with a greater role for emotion and social action than Levi-Strauss seems to provide.

Although Levi-Strauss is critical of Durkheim's emblem theory of totemism, especially of his attempt to derive totems from graphic designs and the emotions associated with them (1963:93, 95–6; 1966:239), he recognizes that names and emblems, as well as food prohibitions, differences in clothing, bodily paintings, and behavior, are some of the ways in which different clans signify their differences (1966:149–50). Moreover, he asserts that each clan "possesses 'a symbol of life' —a totem or divinity— whose name it adopts" (1966:147), and that the totemic animal "is not grasped as a biological entity but as a conceptual tool" (ibid., pp. 148–9). The inedible and distinctive parts of a totemic animal, for example, such as the feathers, beaks, or teeth, may be "adopted as emblems by groups of men in order to do away with their own resemblances" (ibid., pp. 106–8).

Goldenweiser, although not usually considered as presenting a structuralist interpretation (indeed, one cannot find an explicitly structuralist formulation comparable, say, to Radcliffe-Brown's second paper or Levi-Strauss's conception of the homologous two systems of differences), in some respects anticipates Radcliffe-Brown and Levi-Strauss while in other respects goes beyond them both.

In linking a totemic culture to a social organization, subdivided into functionally analogous or equivalent but separate social units, Goldenweiser is close to Radcliffe-Brown as well as to Durkheim. In such a community, "the first demand is for some kind of classifiers, preferably names, which would identify the separate units and yet signify their equivalence by belonging to one category." And, "all along, the classificatory aspect remains a fixed requirement, so whatever traits may develop in the social crucible appear as homologous traits" (Goldenweiser 1918:291). He stresses, as Levi-Strauss does, that "things in nature," and particularly animals, are "constantly used for naming individuals, groups of all varieties, such as families, societies, clubs, game teams, political parties, houses, constellations" because they are homologous in structure to human social groups, and perhaps even more than either Radcliffe-Brown or Levi-Strauss, he clarified how these animals and "things in nature" serving as classifiers become "symbols of the social values of the group (ibid., p. 191, 193). Their very objectivity as well as emotional significance lend themselves readily to artistic elaboration" (ibid., p. 291). Such objects, he explains, are "early drawn into the domain of art—painted, tattooed, carved, woven, embroidered, dramatized in dances; they figure in all realistic as well as geometric representations, thus also rising into prominence as badges, signs and symbols" (ibid., p. 293).[3]

In his explanation, Goldenweiser neither derives the totemic symbolism directly from the social organizaiton, as he believed Durkheim tried to do, nor gives primacy to the cognitive and intellectual factors. He postulates, rather, a mutual "fitness" of the social and cultural aspects of totemism, which are disparate but undergo a "mutual penetration" and "further elaboration" as they interact (1918:290). Through the operation of such a process of mutual adjustment, emotions and attitudes (the totem's cultural content) become "socialized" and the social groups which become associated with the symbols and objects of emotional value are "constituted as definite social units" (Goldenweiser 1910:275; 1918:290–1).

Along with Linton (1924), Sapir (1927), and Kipling (1932), in his poem *The Totem,* Goldenweiser found that the tendencies and processes underlying totemism were also operative in modern society, where "equivalent social units are known to adopt as classifiers names, badges, pins, flags, tattoo marks, colors. One thinks of high school and college classes, baseball and football teams, political parties, the degrees of Elks and Masons, and the regiments of our armies." Totemic emblems and symbols so generated are "charged with potential emotions" (1931:277).

[3]There is an interesting discussion of emblems and symbols in Walter Crane's *The Bases of Design* (1914). Crane, one of the most important late 19th century illustrators and designers, gives a brief but useful history of emblems from the point of view of design principles and gives consideration to the identifying functions as well as to the esthetic forms of emblems (1914:248).

A full and detailed development of the analogy between modern society and totemic rites and beliefs was worked out in Lloyd Warner's "Yankee City" monograph on *The Living and the Dead* (1959). This analogy, it is relevant to note, had already become a topic for comment among some American anthropologists even before Warner started his "Yankee City" research. It is also interesting that Warner, trained at Berkeley in the Boas tradition under Lowie and Kroeber, was prepared to combine culture history and cultural psychology to arrive at conclusions about "cultural dynamics," nevertheless confined his interests in "cultural dynamics" to an appendix of his Murngin book (see Warner 1937). While this may be testimony to his encounter with Radcliffe-Brown and structuralism, it does not entirely explain his return to Durkheim's emblem theory of totemism. That explanation will be found, I believe, in the fact that through the emblem concept Warner achieved a third kind of generalization, beyond the two kinds identified by Leach (1961): Radcliffe-Brown's comparative method ("butterfly collecting") and Levi-Strauss's structuralism ("inspired guesses at mathematical pattern"). The third kind of generalization is that of a semiotic anthropology—a kind not reached for by many other anthropologists until almost a decade later, but which has now become more popular, as Geertz has recently observed:

> The move toward conceiving of social life in terms of symbols . . . whose meaning . . . we must grasp if we are to understand that organization and formulate its principles, has grown by now to formidable proportions. The woods are full of eager interpreters. [Geertz 1980:167.]

3

After Durkheim's *Elementary Forms of the Religious Life* (1915), the next serious application of the emblem theory was Warner's *A Black Civilization* (1937).This monograph, based on three years of fieldwork in Northern Australia (1926–29) under the tutelage of Radcliffe-Brown, focused on the description and interpretation of Murngin totemic institutions and symbolism giving special attention to the role of totemic emblems in funerals and initiation rites, their relations to dances, songs, dramatic rites, and myths, and their social significance (Warner 1937:Chaps. 9–13).

While Warner recognized the need for a general theory of signs and symbols and began to apply Ogden and Richards's semantic triangle to his analysis of Murngin totemism (see Warner 1937:247–8, 407–8), he did not formulate a method and theory for the study of "symbolic life" until a later monograph (see 1959:Part V). In that monograph, *The Living and the Dead,* Warner generalized Durkheim's conception of totemic emblems as collective representations to a semiotic analysis of signs and symbols. Emblems become *symbols* and

> the essential definition of a symbol are the sign and its meaning, the former usually being the outward perceptible form which is culturally identifiable and recognizable, the latter being the interpretation of the sign, usually composed of concepts of what is being interpreted and the positive and negative values and feelings which "cluster about" the sign. The sign's meaning may refer to other objects or express and evoke feelings. The values and feelings may relate to the inner world of the person or be projected outward on the social and natural worlds beyond. [Warner 1959:4.]

Warner's definition of a sign and its meaning is strikingly similar to Peirce's triadic conception of a sign, its object, and its interpretant. Peirce, however, defines "symbol" in a broader sense than Warner, to refer to any sign-type whose meaning is general and depends on some kind of conventional agreement. Whether or not Peirce's semiotic theory was known to Warner is uncertain; it is probable that some of it filtered through such contributors to symbolic theory as G.H. Mead, Ogden and Richards, C.W. Morris, Sapir, Freud, Jung, Pareto, Levi and Frye, Durkheim, Piaget, Radcliffe-Brown, Malinowski, Mauss, and Kluckhohn (see Warner 1959:449–51).

Some influence of each of these theorists is evident in Warner's theory of symbolism. (For examples see Warner 1959:445, 459, 484, Chap. 15 and Singer 1981.) In the present paper, however, we shall not deal primarily with Warner's general theory of symbolism but with how he applied that theory to the emblematic systems in Yankee City in the 1930s and how these systems and the identities they symbolize have been changing in the 1970s.

Warner frequently characterized his studies of Yankee City as being based on the same methods he had used in his Murngin study. Describing the preparations for the 1930 Tercentenary Procession in Yankee City, Warner suggested the arrangement of story and dramatic ceremony provided "a close analogue to the historical myths and rites of a primitive society" which made it possible to utilize similar procedures (1959:116). The interpretation of Yankee City Memorial Day ceremonies as "a cult of the dead organized around the community cemeteries," led him to suggest further that "just as the totemic symbol system of the Australians represents the idealized clan, and the African ancestral worship symbolizes the family and state, so the Memorial Day rites symbolize and express the sentiments of the people for the total community and the state" (ibid., p. 277).

Warner, no doubt, appreciated the shock value of describing a modern community in terms of stone-age rituals and myths. But he had a more serious purpose than culture shock and social satire. He was also willing to read the parallel in reverse and describe Murngin rituals and myths in terms of drama and dance, recreation and play, art, religion, and cosmology. It was not that he wished to flatter his Australian friends but rather, following Radcliffe-Brown, that he believed social anthropology to be a generalizing science which, through the use of the comparative method, would develop a framework of concepts and methods for the study of all societies and cultures.

For both Warner and Radcliffe-Brown, the comparative method depends on the observation of differences as well as resemblances. Therefore, the description and analysis of parallels between Yankee City Memorial Day ceremonies and the Tercentenary Procession and Murngin totemic rituals and myths would need to take account of the more complex culture and society of Yankee City with its diversity of social groups and values and its background of written history. Its identity belongs to several different historical universes at one time (the ever-widening circles of identification from Massachusetts, to New England, the United States of America, Western Culture, and the rest of the world) and its history has to be seen in the context of national and world events as well as in a local perspective (Warner 1959:115–16). It may very well be that Warner's use of the comparative method yields a definition of collective representations and their relations to the social structure that conforms to the definition Durkheim proposed in his classic study of Australian totemism. However, such a result cannot be posited in drawing the parallel; it must be taken as an hypothesis for empirical inquiry.

During our first visits to "Yankee City" we were struck by the prominence given to emblems of identity and related visual and verbal symbols. A local guide pointed out "the Irish Church," "the French Church," "the Greek Orthodox Church," "the Synagogue," and "the Unitarian Church" with its handsome spire. Many participants and members of the audience in the Annual "Yankee Homecoming" celebration dressed in colonial costumes as gentlemen and yeomen, patriots and redcoats. Officers and sailors of the Continental Navy marched in the Jimmy Fund parade in authentic costume, bearing muskets, led by a fife and drum corps and an honor guard carrying a colonial flag with thirteen stars. Early nineteenth century buildings had horse hitches and colonial street lanterns and the partially restored structures in Market Square were draped with flag bunting and marked with antique signs portraying occupations and products for sale.

Our initial impression was that we had come upon a Shakespearean world in which religion, race, and ethnicity, social class and occupation, age and sex were all visibly inscribed in dress and speech, in public and private architecture, and in the façades of buildings and shops. This impression did not survive a closer acquaintance with the community, however, which has been undergoing changes that have blurred the colorful seventeenth and eighteenth century images of the city. Perhaps in the 1930s this image retained enough verisimilitude to persuade young social anthropologist Lloyd Warner that he had found a New England community with a sufficiently well-ordered social system, a long-enough standing cultural tradition, and enough of an old-family Yankee aristocracy to justify reapplying the social anthropological methods he had used earlier to study Australian aborigines.

In fact, one former resident of Yankee City, novelist John P. Mar-

quand, recalled the old social order as still extant in the early 1930s
when Warner and his staff came to study it. By 1960, when his revised
biography of "Lord" Timothy Dexter was published, Marquand wrote
that while the outlines of the society which so interested the Warner
researchers still existed, "it had been altered in many ways beyond
recognition." The town no longer was an isolated community. The
famous Federalist houses along High Street no longer were the same.
Puritan and sophisticated traditions of the past were becoming replaced
by "plastic motifs that give the most authentic part of State Street a
jukebox air" (Marquand 1960:122). Noting the recent publication of
Warner's last Yankee City monograph, *The Living and the Dead,* Marquand suggested that "if Mr. Warner were to continue further with his
Yankee City, another volume might be a very different saga" (ibid.,
pp. 16–17).[4]

Neither Marquand nor Warner ever wrote that different saga. The
chiefly historical reconstruction of the eighteenth century eccentric
merchant, "Lord" Timothy's life and career, was Marquand's last book
about his home city. Warner revised and supplemented *The Living and
the Dead* in *The Family of God* (1961) and also edited a condensed
summary of his five-volume series in *Yankee City* (1963). Yet, it was
the kinds of changes that Marquand was beginning to discern in the
early 1960s that had crystallized by the 1970s when we revisited the
city. A careful reading of Warner's *The Living and the Dead* reveals
anticipations of how the old order was beginning to change even in the
days of "Biggy" Muldoon, Warner's epithet for the colorful populist
mayor. Although that volume can no longer be considered a completely
accurate ethnographic guide to "Yankee City," it remains valid and
highly valuable in two important respects: as a base-line for studying
how the Yankee City of the 1930s has changed, and as a pioneering
innovation in semiotic anthropology.

---

[4] The subject of Marquand's biography, "Lord" Timothy Dexter, is perhaps the
most picturesque example of the "ancestor worship and status strivings" Marquand
describes. Dexter surrounded his famous mansion on High Street with about 40 carved
wooden statues of former presidents, Napoleon and other "greats," animals and god-
desses, and a statue of himself labeled "I am the first in the East, the first in the West,
and the greatest Philosopher in the Western World" (Marquand 1960:265).

If, indeed, the New England urban community studied by Warner and his researchers in the 1930s can no longer be represented by the traditional emblems (of ethnicity, race, and religion, or of social class, occupation, age, and sex), then why does it give visitors the impression that it is still a Shakespearean world? And how have these emblems of identity changed in the 1970s?

In the course of our revisits to Yankee City, we met several inhabitants who spontaneously expressed appreciation for Warner's account of Memorial Day celebrations in *The Living and the Dead* or in *The Family of God*. They felt the description was accurate, and also believed the account captured the occasion's spirit and what it meant to their families and the community. The contrast with contemporary Memorial Day celebrations heightened their appreciation since these were no longer well-attended community-wide ceremonies.

Although few commented on Warner's comparison of Memorial Day with Australian totemism, this analogy, if not completely persuasive, is easiest to trace in his description and interpretation of Memorial Day as an "American Sacred Ceremony." Chapters 8 and 9 ("The Symbolic Relations of the Dead and the Living" and "The City of the Dead" respectively) in *The Living and the Dead* obviously correspond to Chapters XII and XIII (on "Mortuary Rites" and their Interpretation) in *Black Civilization*. Furthermore there is a deeper correspondence in the structure, organization, and functions of the rituals and ceremonies the effect of which is to remedy the injuries to the living inflicted by death and to restore the solidarity of the community weakened by loss of some members.

The basic outlines of Warner's theory derive from Durkheim and Van Gennep (1959:278, 303, 402). His detailed application of the theory to Memorial Day ceremonies is original and most ingenious in showing how varied social groups and associations, including ethnic groups who are otherwise excluded from participation in community activities, are incorporated into the ceremonies. The Memorial Day rites of Yankee City, and of other American towns, represent a modern "cult of the dead " that "dramatically express the sentiments of unity of all the living among themselves, of all the living with the dead, and of all the living and the dead as a group with God" (ibid., pp. 278–9).

> Throughout the Memorial Day rites we see people who are
> religiously divided as Protestant, Catholic, Jewish, and
> Greek Orthodox participating in a common ritual in a grave-
> yard with their common dead. Their sense of autonomy was
> present and expressed in the separate ceremonies, but the
> parade and unity of doing everything at one time emphasized
> the oneness of the total group. [Warner 1959:268.]

In his analysis of the ceremonies, Warner found that the graves of
the dead were "the most powerful of the visible emblems" unifying
all the groups of the community (Warner 1959:279). He interpreted
the cemetery and its graves as both "a physical emblem" and as "a
social emblem." The several material symbols in the cemetery—such
as the walks, fences, hedges that marked its physical limits, the stone
markers on individual graves, the surnames of the owners on individual
graves, and the landscaping—establish the cemetery as "an enduring
physical emblem, a substantial and visible symbol of this agreement
among men that they will not let each other die" (ibid., p. 285).

As a *social emblem,* the cemetery, according to Warner, provides
for a number of social functions that are continuously renewed by
funerals and other rituals. These functions include disposal of the
corpse and a firm and fixed social place for anchoring the disturbed
sentiments about the dead, "where the living can symbolically maintain
and express their kinship with the dead." The marked grave, Warner
pointed out, is not merely a symbol that "refers generally and abstractly
to all the dead" but is something that belongs to a separate personality.
Thus as a social emblem, the cemetery is "composed of many autonomous and separate individual symbols which give visible expression
to our social relations, to the supernatural and to the pure realm of the
spirit"; yet the cemetery as a sign is whole and entire (Warner
1959:286).

Warner's interpretation of the cemetery as a set of both physical
and social emblems obviously generalizes the concept of emblems to
embrace a variety of material symbols and their varied social functions.
How such symbols become emblems of identity and of whom or what
they emblematize he explained through the analogy of the cemetery
with "a city of the dead." This metaphorical designation was derived

from a hymn, "City of Our Dead," used during Memorial Day religious services. Through intensive observations of several cemeteries and through interviews, he and his co-workers collected enough data to support his interpretation that the cemeteries are

> the symbolic replica of the living community. . . . The social and status structures which organize the living community of Yankee City are vividly and impressively reflected and expressed in the outward forms and internal arrangements of the several cemeteries in the city. [Warner 1959:286-7.]

The location of graves within a cemetery, the number, size, and location of headstones, the kind of stone borders, carvings, and inscriptions indicated to Warner and his staff the differences between elementary and extended families, the changing mobility of a family and the relative status of family members according to age and sex. Ethnic, religious, and associational affiliations were also indicated by similar markers and by the use of distinctive emblems on the graves— such as the insignia of the American Legion, the Elks and Moose, the cross and lamb for Catholic Christians, and the greater use of the American flag for the graves of ethnic groups.

Warner noted the dual character of the symbolism on the ethnic graves which included inscriptions in English as well as in the ethnic language, headstones and wooden crosses on the same grave, and an American flag together with a small replica of a house with wax flowers and a candle inside. In addition, he observed that the dual symbolism was more prominent among families of more recent immigrants.

4

In *The Living and the Dead,* Warner pointed out that only six out of the eleven cemeteries were decorated on Memorial Day, that the rest were neglected because their dead had no living representatives (1959:319). This observation led him to suggest the interesting idea that cemeteries "die" and cease to exist as "sacred emblems" when members no longer take care of the graves or bury their dead there. Such cemeteries, however, become "historical monuments" over time: their gravestones become "artifacts and symbols that refer to the past." They no longer symbolize a man's death, or evoke man's hope for immortality, but only that he and others "once lived and constituted a way of life and a society." The living "lose their feelings for social continuity and the social character of the graveyard and its sacred character," although they may recognize it as an object of historical significance (ibid., p. 319).

While "dead" cemeteries have lost their sacred character and have become historical symbols they still retain value for the community as collective representations expressing feelings for both the past and the dead. For example, in the 1970s, high school students were recruited to work in one of these historic cemeteries—weeding, polishing and restoring the gravestones, marking boundaries, and the like—but not to express respect for their own ancestors, for most of them were not buried in that cemetery. Rather, it was, in part, an effort to help the students and others learn more about the community's history.

Warner's distinction between the "sacred emblems" of living cemeteries and the "historical symbols" in dead cemeteries is the key to the difference between his analysis of the Memorial Day ceremonies and his analysis of the celebration of the Tercentenary of the Massachusetts Bay Colony. The former deals largely with the physical and social sacred emblems of the dead, the past of the species, and the future of the individual; while the latter deals largely with the past and present secular symbols of the living. The polarity of sacred and secular symbols also plays a role in Warner's interpretation of other calendrical and life-cycle rituals and in the discussion of religious beliefs and practices; but the contrast emerges most sharply when he compares Memorial Day with the Tercentenary (Warner 1959:5, 103). In his analysis of the Tercentenary, Warner found it necessary to introduce a concept of "secular ritualization" to parallel the ritual of sacred legitimation. In *Yankee City* (1961), he explains, "the souls of the ancestors cannot be called up ritually from the past to live in the present as they are in totemic rites of simpler peoples . . . something else needs to be done" (1961:104). That something else, for Warner, was a series of secular rituals which appealed to the authority of scientific history and to the arts and crafts of historical reconstruction to legitimize the version of the past presented in the Tercentenary:

> The people of Yankee City, mostly Protestant and all skeptics in that they live in a modern, science-based civilization, must settle for less—if not the souls of the ancestors, then at least images evoking for the living the spirit that animated the generations that embodied the power and glory of yesterday. [Warner 1961:104.]

There is no question that the imagery of the Tercentenary as Warner describes it in *The Living and the Dead* (part II) and as independently checked by our own research, was evocative of the spirit of past power and glory. The paintings and pictures of sculptured models for the floats, living actors in tableaux with historic costumes and settings, and the representations of George Washington, Lafayette, along with local "greats," evoked from participants and audience alike just those sentiments that Durkheim had said were inspired by the "glorious souvenirs" that are "made to live again before their eyes and with which they feel they have a kinship" (Durkheim 1947:375).

The Tercentenary Committee placed over a hundred historical markers at selected houses, churches, cemeteries, at historic spots on roads and rivers, at the harbour, and on public buildings. These plaques testified to the great interest in historical factuality and authenticity, which Warner pointed out and which still prevails.[5]

The need for "secular ritualization" in the Tercentenary may not have been as great as Warner supposed, for, as he himself pointed out, a "large proportion of the people are now ethnic, including Catholic Irish, Jews, French-Canadians, Greeks, Poles and others" (Warner

---

[5] Warner refers to many of the objects identified by the historical markers as "symbols" or "emblems." See especially his discussion of the historic cemeteries (1959:265–70, 280–7); the old houses and furnishings, paintings and gardens (1959:44–50, 114, 151–5); and of sailing ships (1959:48–9, 140–2, 208).

1959:151). Under these conditions neither iconoclasm nor skepticism was necessarily a dominant obstacle to belief and faith in the Tercentenary's historical images and symbols.

Warner maintained his contention that the Yankee City Tercentenary Procession was a secular ritual in which patently religious symbols and figures were given a purely historical and secular interpretation even for those floats that referred to Puritan fathers, among them Governor John Winthrop:

> The symbols, officially and in fact, were referential; their signs were marks that pointed to events of the Puritan past. But nowhere in the entire pageant was there any sacred sign which demanded an act of faith about a sacred world past. . . . The whole celebration was cast in rationalistic terms; all super-naturalism was suppressed. [Warner 1959:213.]

Although the Puritans "in their own self-conceptions were a holy people directed by God in his Word, the Bible," Warner found that "the Bible, whose words carry different meanings for each of the churches, had no part in the general collectivity's pageant rites" (Warner 1959:215). This passage is followed by a cryptic sentence which may well hide significant exceptions to Warner's negative generalization:

> Only in the sermons of the churches and a brief collective ceremony at a hill beyond the dwellings of the town after the celebration was over were the Bible and the sacred world allowed to enter the symbolism of the Tercentenary. [Warner 1959:215.]

Judging from our observations in the 1970s, when some of the churches held ecumenical services before, during, and after such historical reenactments as the Battle of Bunker Hill, it seems reasonable to assume that the Bible and the sacred world were allowed to enter the Tercentenary's symbolism. It may have been true, as Warner explained, that the need for unity in a religiously diverse community "drives the markers and meanings of sacred life into the confined contexts of each church, for some to the brief, unimportant ceremony on the hill" (1959:215). However, the marks and meanings of these boundaries between religious and secular rites were probably not as sharply defined as he suggested.

There is some indirect evidence in Warner's account for the proposition that the Catholic and other non-Protestant ethnic participants in the Tercentenary had no difficulty responding to religious and secular symbolism combined. This evidence comes from a dichotomy between the visual symbolism of Catholic rituals and the verbal symbolism of Protestant rituals (Warner 1959:306–8, 332–6). The visual symbols, according to Warner, involve all the senses and the whole body; they consist of form, shape, color, texture, movement, and rhythm. Because they readily excite the emotions and the imagination, they are "non-logical" and tap deep organic and psychological needs. The verbal symbols—chiefly the words of sermons, prayers, and hymns—he believed, reduced the sacred and spiritual symbols of mental life to "an arbitrary mechanical alphabet." The poverty of symbolic expression, akin to "the cold, alien rationality of science," drives the "lower orders" to look for "compensatory substitutes" in "ecstatic emotional outbursts" for "the satisfactions they once felt in church rituals" (ibid., pp. 335–6).

The context of Warner's distinction between visual and verbal symbols is a discussion of sacred religious symbols and rites such as the Mass for Catholics and sermons, prayers, and hymns for Protestants. His analysis of the response to visual symbolism, however, should hold as well for the response to the pageantry, costumes, shapes, colors, and textures of the Tercentenary, even where symbols and figures of religious significance are excluded. On the Protestant side, Warner himself points out that the laic liturgy has been changing towards a greater recognition of the symbols of family, women, and of organic needs and functions (Warner 1959: 391–5; 1961:75). He interprets Mother's Day, for example, as "a Return of the Woman and Her Family to the Protestant Pantheon" (1959:343).

Warner interpreted the trends of change in Protestant liturgy, probably observed on a revisit to Yankee City in the 1950s, as a reversal of the alleged impoverishment of religious rites and symbolism from the Protestant Revolt and Puritanism. In this respect, at least, the liturgical revival is also a return to the seventeenth century which Mario Praz calls an age of emblems (an externalization of the image by plastic interpretation), an age of opera (when things are said and represented at the same time, according to Diderot), and an age of allegorical tableaux, when words were "made intelligible by being diagrammatically related to one another—an age when a verbal culture was being transmuted into a visual culture" (Praz 1964:15). (Praz cites W.J. Ong's article, "From Allegory to the Diagram in the Renaissance Mind," published in 1959 as a source for his formulation.)

5

Warner's interpretation of the identities asserted by the display of flags and other emblems on Yankee City graves or by the colonial uniforms and insignia worn in the Tercentenary Procession is, at one level, quite transparent. This is especially true if the interpretation is based not only on the description of isolated emblems, but also on interviews with the participants in the ceremonies and an analysis of their social and cultural contexts. Given the kind of social and cultural context usually described in Warner's analysis, distinctions such as he makes between "physical emblems" and "social emblems," or between "sacred emblems" and "secular symbols," become rather subtle but can be checked by other kinds of data. These distinctions depend on a constellation of factors including the graphic design of the emblem and its context of use, the users' intentions and the observers' perceptions, local customs and social structure. These are the kinds of considerations Warner took into account when he wrote that ethnic graves displayed more American flags than "native" graves because the ethnic families wished to symbolize that their deceased relative either was a citizen or intended to become one, while the custom among "native" families was to place flags only on the graves of soldiers.

In addition to such considerations underlying Warner's and other anthropologists' interpretations of emblems there are, I believe, usually some assumptions about the kind of social and cultural universe symbolized by a set of emblems, and about the different kinds of people whose identities are emblematized. In our initial impression of Yankee City, for example, we tended to assume that it was a kind of Shakespearean world in which individuals, families, and social classes, ethnic, religious and social groups are clearly identified by distinctive emblems and names. These impressions were in part the afterglow, as Marquand observed, of the old social order that was still extant in Yankee City in the 1930s when Warner and his staff came to study it. That the old social order had begun to change beyond recognition by the early 1960s was not immediately reflected in the symbolism of emblems and names. In fact, it is astonishing to find so much of Yankee City's old order emblematized and identified in Warner's last monograph, *The Living and the Dead:* the six social classes; the opposition between "Yankees" and "Ethnics"; the Federalist houses, gardens, associated streets, and neighborhoods as status symbols; the superior prestige of "old families" who can trace their genealogies to the Federalist period of power and glory; and the emphasis on the Protestant and Puritan revolt as a source of the city's long-established cultural and religious traditions. The first evidence of change comes at the beginning of this monograph in the story of "Biggy" Muldoon (actually "Bossy" Gillis); the colorful 1930s Irish mayor whose dramatic assault on a Federalist house and the Yankee establishment it symbolized. This included the prominent display of circus posters on the exterior of the house and the erection of mock-headstones in the garden to protest an unfavorable zoning ruling against the mayor made by the city council, and marked for many the opening blow against the old social order. Two other instances of change appear in his descriptions of how the "mobile elite" acquired houses with long-established "lineages," and of "a liturgical renaissance" among the Protestant churches (Warner 1959:17-18).

Such evidences of change, however, did not swamp Warner. He believed he had found in the Memorial Day Ceremonies, in the Tercentenary Procession, and in other sacred and secular rites, evidences for the survival of the great tradition—its sacred dead, famous heroes, historic battles, sailing ships, grand houses, faraway places, and peoples with whom they traded. The symbolic representations of these events, objects, people and places in the form of emblems, names, and other symbols were encapsulated in the cultural performances Warner observed and analyzed. The parallels he drew with the totemic rites and myths of Australian aborigines were not so much intended to demonstrate the primitiveness of a New England urban community; rather, the purpose of these parallels, for Warner as for Durkheim, was to suggest a method for discovering the values, cosmology, and history of an entire society and a culture.

During our revisits to "Yankee City" in the 1970s we found many of the same emblems, symbols, and themes Warner described for the 1930s. In the annual nine-day "Yankee Homecoming" events, in the Bicentennial celebrations of 1976, in the restoration of historic houses on High Street, and in the church services and sermons one could recognize visual and verbal, secular and sacred symbols from the "Yankee City" of the 1930s—eagles, flags, fifes and drums, colonial dress and uniforms, historic reenactments, prayers, and hymns. While, to be sure, there are some differences in the symbolism of the 1970s, the similarities are nevertheless sufficiently numerous and striking to evoke the initial impression of a city that is still recognizably the same as the one Warner described. Can we conclude from our shock of recognition that "Yankee City's" constellation of emblems and symbols denote or connote the same identities—ethnic, racial, religious, social, national, and local—that Warner found in the 1930s? Such a conclusion seems doubtful for reasons that will be discussed below.

If our first impression of "Yankee City" was of a kind of Shakespearean world in which "Yankees" and "Ethnics" wore their emblems of identity on their houses, shops, and churches—if not on their clothes and tabards—it soon gave way to a second impression haunted by the question, where have all the "Yankees" and the "Ethnics" gone? Among the Federalist and other old houses along High Street we found only one old Yankee family still living in their ancestral home out of only about twenty Yankee families living there at all (*cf.* Warner 1959:114, 152, 154). Death, moving away, and lack of children and grandchildren have decreased their numbers. They have been displaced by Irish, Greek, French-Canadian, Jewish, and Indian householders, doctors, and prosperous young professionals.

A similar shift in the relative composition of "Yankees" and "Ethnics" was also found in the organizing committees for "Yankee Homecoming," Bicentennial activities and restoration, educational and public service groups. These committees, no longer dominated by "Yankees" as they were in the 1930s, according to Warner, were now controlled by "Ethnics" or "former Ethnics." A sprinkling of ethnic surnames even appeared among the officers and membership lists of such citadels of Yankee tradition and family as the Historical Society and the Sons and Daughters of the First Settlers.

It was often pointed out during our visits that the city was run by an informal establishment including the then mayor, a newspaper editor, a banker, an insurance company director, and a lawyer. Only one of these five members of the establishment came from a local old Yankee family; the others came from second or third generation "ethnic" families.

As significant as the changing relative status of "Yankees" and "Ethnics" is, the changes in the verbal categories and designations are perhaps more significant. Terms like "Yankees" and "Ethnics" are no longer popular or current. The city clerk reported that because most people so vigorously resist answering questions about ethnicity, religion, race, income, and social class he has had to drop these questions from the political registration cards, and list only name, address, age, and occupation. He was angered, along with other clerks, by a recent tendency for some parents to select surnames of choice for both their children and themselves. Although the State Supreme Court has ruled that this is a matter of family life protected by the First Amendment, the clerk believed it would create a "colossal mess" in various types of records involving names. In addition, this practice would tend to shake the heavy reliance people place on surnames as a source of information about ethnicity, religion, and race. Although such inferences from surnames are often guesswork, surnames are becoming the last surviving symbolism of the old social order.

Currently, even the popular designations of the churches are changing. The "Irish Church" and the "French Church" are beginning to lose their former interpretations. While a priest in charge of the Church of the Immaculate Conception argued that most (about 90% of 6000) church members are Irish, he didn't like the name "the Irish Church":

> We like to say it is American or Catholic. The oldtimers
> still call it the Irish Church but we're all Americans
> here. . . . We're all Catholic, we're all Christians here.
> (Interview 1977.)

The priest at St. Louis de Gonzague, the "French Church," estimated
that about half of his congregation (of 350 families) was French and
the other half "no longer really French" but a mixture of French and
either Irish, Yankee, or Polish. In the past four years, the priest said,
with regret, he has conducted only two marriages in which both people
were French. Now, with the school gone, he explained, "There is no
means to transmit the language. Everyone is typically American."
(Interview 1977.)

It is tempting to characterize the changing relative status of "Yankees" and "Ethnics" and the associated demographic and symbolic
changes, as a transformation from a Yankee-dominated identity to an
ethnic-dominated identity with a persistence of the old emblems. Such
a characterization, however, would run counter to several important
groups of facts. One fact is that many people feel unsure about their
identities and are constantly looking for them through genealogical,
historical, and archaeological research. Their desire to validate their
authenticity seems as obsessive now as it was, according to Warner's
observations, in the 1930s (Singer 1977). This is as true of many
"Yankees" as it is of "Ethnics." At the same time, the very categories
of "Yankee" and "Ethnic" are becoming blurred in definition and use,
while the old ethnic epithets are being strenuously avoided in public.
A member of an authentic Yankee family, for example, said he would
not consider his neighbor who was a Polish immigrant and farmer, a
"Yankee," but the farmer's locally born son would qualify as one. In
another case, a third generation resident of Hungarian descent would
not call himself a "Yankee," but considered his young daughter one
because his wife was a "Yankee." His wife disagreed. She insisted the
daughter would be considered "Hungarian-American" adding that her
own pedigree included some Irish and Scotch as well as Yankee.

There is a definite trend to broaden the definition of "Yankee" to
include anyone born in New England and to avoid such terms as

"ethnic," "native," and "foreigner." One local Yankee, a descendant from English ancestors who was himself something of a historian, maintained that "Yankee" was what the French called the English and derived from *L'Anglais d'eau douce*. Ironically, a second-generation ethnic maintained that the only "natives" were the American Indians. One Black family (partly of American Indian descent) formally traced the husband's descent from a French ancestor, but also regularly attended tribal get-togethers with their Mashpee relatives and travelled to see other American Indians in various parts of the country.

Amidst the cross-currents of changing usage and shifting definitions the fact that the United States Census for 1970 gives 76% "native of native parentage" for Yankee City, is a justification for calling it a "Yankee City." This figure might be compared to Warner's figures of 45% ethnic and 55% Yankee, although such figures and comparisons have serious limitations. A number of "natives of native parentage" did not consider themselves "Yankees" and were not so called because they were of "ethnic" descent. Warner's "ethnics," on the other hand, included only 36% foreign born and 64% native born; 42% in Yankee City, 20% in the rest of New England, and 2% in the rest of the United States. Of the "natives," 280 or about 8½% were foreign born and mainly of English, North Irish and Scottish descent (Warner 1963:2–4; Warner and Lunt 1941:220–21).

The terms "oldtimer" and "newcomer" suggest another significant trend in usage. While these are long-standing designations, they are being used to mark a new kind of phenomenon. One family, for example, of 17th century English descent with one parent related to "old" and respected Boston Brahmins, who had lived and had children born in "Yankee City" over 40 years, was still regarded as "new-comers" and "outsiders." Another family, however, whose father's parents had immigrated to Yankee City from Greece, was considered to be "oldtimers." According to Warner's definition, they were "Eth-nics" and would have remained so for five or six generations. These contrasting usages, which were widespread, are significant because they indicate a speeding-up and, possibly, a reversal of Warner's pre-dicted "time-table for assimilation" (Warner 1963:Chap. 14; Warner and Srole 1942:Chap. 10). Perhaps they are even more significant in indicating the replacement or displacement of the older "Yankee-Eth-nic" opposition. To paraphrase Levi-Strauss, one system of differences based on race, religion, ethnicity, and social class is being transformed into another system of differences based on local birth, duration of local residence, community acceptance, and lifestyle (*cf.* Schneider 1969, 1979).

Lifestyle is not defined in terms of Warner's social classes or of mobility within the system, but rather in terms of such polarities as "workingmen" and "intellectuals," "straights" and "Third World oriented." One leading local banker told me there were only two classes, not six, in the city and he himself was a workingman. The city clerk described the "intellectuals" as coming from Harvard or Marblehead in their red M.G.s and trying to tell the "oldtimers" how to run the city.

Some of these characterizations have been crystallized in recent years by disputes over urban renewal and restoration, and over the use of living space by arts and crafts people. The group pushing for conventional urban renewal, it turned out, were "oldtimers" and "workingmen," while those supporting restoration and preservation were "newcomers," "outsiders," and "intellectuals."

The arts and crafts people are "newcomers" and "outsiders" who neither affiliate with the "intellectuals" nor the "workingmen" because they see their own lifestyle as distinctive. Most are without professional positions and incomes, or permanent residence and acceptance in the community; they regard themselves as an enclave of expatriates from the 1960s. Commenting on a midnight inspection tour by city officials of their loft-like studios in an old warehouse building where some of the craftsmen and their families also illegally resided, one of the crafts people explained the "raid" as "a clash of lifestyles: crafting and artistry is opting for a lifestyle rather than an income level, and that right there separates people who are into a different reason for having jobs. . . . There's a communication gap right there, a little suspicion." (The official reason for the night inspection was fire-prevention and enforcement.)

The range of work in arts and crafts is quite broad—in addition to painting, drawing, and photography, there are craftsmen in all the traditional media and in several media that are new: batik and raku, metalwork, woodwork, weaving, stitchery and macrame, glass, enamel, porcelain, and stoneware are all represented. The themes of their work are unusual and significant in at least one respect: they tend to avoid the racial, religious, and ethnic typing and the historical portraits that were so prominent in the 1930 Boston Art Exhibition (Boston Tercentenary). While non-representational art is well represented, local scenes as well as historical and contemporary restorations are widely available in post cards, posters, signs, drawings, and paintings. One nationally acclaimed ceramic artist produced a series of porcelain "puzzle pictures" of city buildings and shapes called "A Touch of Gold" which refers to the gilt edge outlining some of the pictures and probably to a satirical comparison with Rockport and Glouchester.

The passing of the old social order in which the opposition between "Yankees" and "Ethnics" was the most salient symbolism has been publicly recognized and discussed. In 1976, several features and editorials in the city's leading newspaper attributed the progress and influence of the ethnic groups to their abandonment of the crude confrontation tactics of a "Bossy" Gillis and to the "maturation" of the second and third generations. The grammar schools and high schools, their teachers, the baseball field, and the corner grocery store were singled out as important stimulators to the process whereby "ethnics" matured into "oldtimers." This view was confirmed in my interviews with members of three-generation families, allowing for individual, family, and other group variations. While over the seventy- or eighty-year careers of the three-generation families many incidents of struggle, frustration, poverty, and discrimination were occasionally remembered (compare T. White's similar recollections of his childhood in Boston), the overall picture described was one of successful acculturation, moderate prosperity, and community acceptance. In sum, the process of "maturation" was telescoped and smoothed out through recollecting.

Another explanation for the smoothness of the "maturation" process, offered by the more articulate and thoughtful individuals (including members of the establishment), included such factors as the traditional tolerance of a seaport city engaged in world trade, the relatively small numbers of most of the ethnic groups represented, and the more liberal and democratic attitudes that soldiers brought back from the Second World War and the Korean War.

The "maturation" and acceptance of the different ethnic groups has not yet resulted in the complete disappearance of their ethnic identity; although many of these families have become quite acculturated, especially in the third generation, they do not always feel completely assimilated. In our visits to their homes, we noted an interesting symbolic expression of this sense of persisting ethnic identity: emblems of their ethnic identity were usually displayed in a kind of counterpoint with emblems of their American identity. This dual symbolism seems to recall Warner's observations of the 1930s cemeteries, except the domestic symbolism of the 1970s has a different meaning and function.

One family of Italian descent, for example, who had lived at least three generations in "Yankee City," displayed two sets of portraits on their living room walls: one set of Michaelangelo-like drawings of a man and a woman, and one set of painted portraits, probably early nineteenth century, of a man and a woman. Both the drawings and the paintings were bought in an antique shop. In another home, a young man of Hungarian descent and of the third generation displayed a crewel work in Hungarian made by his grandmother, as well as an English Renaissance portrait symbolizing his wife's ancestry also hung on the wall.

Other examples include: a small segment of a genealogical chart that traced a wife's Yankee ancestry to 1620 which hung on the wall in another house while an Indian scupture of Krishna and Buddha stood in the garden symbolizing her Indian husband's background; a black couple who showed us pictures of the husband's Mashpee Indian relatives in native American dress, together with pictures of a French forebear who married into the family in 1865 and gave the present patronym, a Bicentennial certificate with the French surname printed on it, and a coat of arms with the surname; the grandfather of a prominent local family who emigrated from Greece had on his walls beside family pictures of his Greek relatives and of his American son and grandchildren, a painting of the Church of Saint Sophia, a Greek Orthodox Church Calendar, and ceramic plates showing the Parthenon, ancient Greek soldiers, Dionysus' sailing boat, and dolphins; another member of a Greek-American family, in addition to many family pictures and Greek ceramics, had on her writing desk a picture of her parents next to a handsome 19th century volume of Byron's poetry. A large pictorial piece of needlepoint showing a Greek shepherd and shepherdess with a flock of sheep hung on one of her walls; and an Armenian grandfather displayed with his family pictures of children and grandchildren and old country relatives, a painstaking and striking picture of a well-known Armenian church which he had constructed from small pieces of wood inlay.

In some of these homes—especially the Greek, Armenian, French-Canadian—the number of family pictures is quite striking. Family size has obviously decreased from the first generation (with fifteen to twenty members) to the third generation (with four to five members), and the increased stress on individual portraits of the grandchildren is evident.

The dual or triple symbolism of the domestic emblem does not imply a conflict between an ethnic and an American identity and our interviews rarely revealed expressions of such a conflict, even among the most self-consciously ethnic families. Rather, the emblematic decorations seemed to be expressions of their desire to be reminded of another identity; one that was either almost forgotten or one that was being revived or newly acquired. The reminders were usually in the form of such artistic constructions as a Chagall-like drawing or print of a reading rabbi with a pigeon overhead, a painting of a Scandinavian fisherman, or the "house-lineage" and early picture of a famous Federalist mansion on High Street.

In the houses of some of the old Yankee families the dual symbolism is less obvious, although documents, portraits, and antiques showing English ancestry are evident. In one home, the framed documents on the walls included a 1773 sampler recording a family birth in 1759 and a bill showing the business dealing of another family member with the eighteenth century merchant, Timothy Dexter. While not quite equivalent to churinga stones, these are "glorious souvenirs" for that family and many others in Yankee City. Some of these items are even being given or loaned to the new Maritime Museum housed in an old Greek-revival customs building, with its "Marquand Room."

6

The following description of the Tercentenary Procession appears in *The Living and the Dead:*

> The themes of the great ethnic migration and their assimi-
> lation—the melting pot, the Promised Land, and the goddess
> of Liberty welcoming them—democracy for all and every
> kind of race and creed—such themes were nowhere present.
> Indeed those who conceived and presented the pageant saw
> themselves as teachers initiating the new peoples into the
> true significance of the nation. [Warner 1959:198.]

This statement may come as a surprise to those who recall Warner's emphasis on the aggregational and integrative functions of the Memorial Day and Tercentenary ceremonies in which the diverse ethnic, religious, racial groups of the city were represented. The statement also seems inconsistent with the trends of change noted for the 1970s, especially the displacement of the "Yankee-Ethnic" opposition into an "oldtimer-newcomer" opposition, and the "maturation" of "ethnics" into "oldtimers" and even "Yankees." The apparent conflicts can be resolved if we take account of some of Warner's assumptions and definitions. In the first place, he assumed that "Yankee City" in the 1930s had a stable social order with a long-standing cultural tradition dominated by "Yankees." Given such an assumption, it was quite plausible to further assume that integrative ceremonies such as Memorial Day and the Tercentenary would not change the social order or alter the dominant cultural traditions. To the extent that some changes deviated from the stable social order and cultural traditions—and Warner described at least one such change in "Biggy" Muldoon's attack on "High Street" and the "Yankee" establishment—the eventual result, Warner predicted, would not be a melting-pot fusion of the different ethnic groups but a gradual transmutation of ethnic elements into a system "almost homogeneous" with the American social system (Warner and Srole 1945:155).

The transmutation of ethnic groups would result in a system not quite homogeneous with the American social system for three reasons,

to interpret Warner and Srole: (1) some ethnic groups became acculturated, lost their distinctive ethnic traits and no longer participated
in the ethnic life of their ancestors yet were not completely accepted
and assimilated; (2) they climbed the social ladder, beginning at the
bottom, but never entered into the "upper upper" class; and (3) some
retained their ethnic ways as a result of the influence of their fathers
and partly because they were not accepted (1945:32).

From these processes of adjustment and transmutation Warner
extrapolated "a time-table for assimilation" for the different ethnic
groups based on their affinity to the "Yankees" in race, religion, and
nationality. Those groups similar to the white, Anglo-Saxon, Protestants will assimilate in a generation or less and those that are different
will take as many as six or more generations, or perhaps never (Warner
1963:Chap. 14).

The ethnic group's structural place in the community and its social
status and rank were not the only criteria, however, that determined
the choice of which float to sponsor in the Tercentenary Procession.
Other criteria included the "symbolic congruence" of the floats' meanings to the sponsor and to others and the "historical significance" of
the symbol and the group (Warner 1959:198). Warner cites the Knights
of Columbus choice of the Columbus float as "multi-determined by
several identifications" including the identity of name, group, and
hero. Despite the fact that "there was no direct connection of the local
association with the person for which the symbol stood," Columbus's
standing as the "first" European to land in America, and the prestige
of the Knights of Columbus made the float choice appropriate in terms
of structural place, symbolic congruence, and historical significance.

A more problematic choice was made by two Jewish representatives
on the Procession's Central Committee. They first agreed to have the
Jewish community sponsor a float for Benedict Arnold who was a local
hero, despite his later reputation as a traitor. This selection was considered inappropriate by the members of the Jewish community and
was changed to sponsorship of Captain John Smith's float. Warner
agreed that for the Jewish community to sponsor the Benedict Arnold
float was inappropriate:

> The Jews could not really afford to sponsor such a symbol;
> their own self-regard and the respect and esteem they needed
> from others would not permit it. . . . Had one of the old
> Yankee organizations or one from the old-family upper class
> sponsored the float, the meaning of the *expedition* would
> have become paramount in the symbols and the meaning of
> Arnold, while prominent, would have been absorbed in the
> larger context. [Warner 1959:203.]

That the float for "The First Class of Harvard" should have been
sponsored by the local Harvard Club or the floats for oldtime shoe-
making and early silversmiths, by those industries, Warner considered
obvious and appropriate identifications. But it was in the sponsorship
of the float for the landing of the first settlers by an historical association
called The Sons and Daughters of the First Settlers that Warner found
the greatest congruence between emblem and sponsors

> in terms of the ultimate identifications and belongingness,
> the Sons and Daughters of the First Settlers of old Yankee
> City who sponsored their own ancestors, the first founders,
> had a collective symbol to represent them to the whole col-
> lectivity which satisfied all the criteria. It said—and they
> and the community said—that they completely belonged,
> and they were so identified. [Warner 1959:199–200.]

In the summer of 1976, a director of The Sons and Daughters of
the First Settlers invited us to their 49th annual gathering. We hesitated
about going after one of our local friends, a "native" and "oldtimer,"
told us that since she was not a descendant of the early settlers, she
would only go to the morning meeting and not to the lunch: she didn't
want to interfere with the "mysteries." We finally gathered up enough
courage to go to the afternoon program, an unveiling of a new bronze
model of the Mary and John, the ship that brought the early settlers
to America. The original model, dedicated in 1905, that "added an
authentic fillip to the sturdy Ancestor Monument on the lower green"
of Old Town was stolen in the autumn of 1974 ("Program" 1976).

The night before the restoration and rededication of the John and Mary, I dreamed of an unveiling of my own which foreshadowed the mood of an incident on the lower green and gave me new insight into "ultimate identifications" and "belongingness." The rededication program on the lower green was pleasant and marked by a spirit of friendliness and good feeling. Some of it, especially the group singing, even evoked assembly hall gatherings in grammar school. It began with a medley of American folk music played on a small electric piano and included "When I First Came to This Land," "This Land is Your Land," and "Yankee Doodle." Then, after greetings from the President, introduction of platform guests, and a prayer of dedication, the bronze model of the Mary and John was unveiled by the sculptor and the oldest member of the society—a local amateur historian, traveller, and former banker in his nineties who later made a short speech that began with Shakespeare's "There are Tides in the Affairs of Men." The model had been wrapped in a French tricolor for reasons not altogether clear except that the President of the Society had been to France during the summer and brought the flag back with him. (He also had a French name and was a teacher of French in the local high school.)

After the unveiling, there was group singing of the first two verses of "America the Beautiful" followed by the presentation of the Mary and John to the town, its acknowledgement and acceptance. The ceremonies closed with group singing of the first three verses of "America," the Benediction, and noted in the program as "Music to Leave by," Woody Guthrie's "So Long, It's been Good to Know You."

As the gathering was beginning to break up one man, not yet a member of The Sons and Daughters, explained to me that his wife had recently applied and that the Society's requirements for genealogical proof of descent from early settlers were very rigorous and difficult to meet, since the early court records had been burned. There were some old apothecary records, but he doubted that these were sufficient to identify a descendant. He then began to ask me some questions. Did I have any ancestors in the area? When I told him no, that I was descended from Abraham, Isaac, and Jacob, he said, "Yes, but to which *local* family are you related?" That I was a visitor from the Midwest did not satisfy him. "Everyone has to come to the United

States by way of New England," he insisted. After I told him that my parents went directly to the Midwest through New York, he recalled that his wife's maternal relatives had also gone directly from New York to the West.

The Society's printed program included two lists of members, one list of 43 "members" with the names of ancestors or of immediate relatives attached, and another list of 118 "members" without any ancestral names attached. A list of 59 "non-members," chiefly from the immediate area, was also included. The then President of the United States, Gerald Ford, was listed as an "honorary member," since the Society's research had found him to be among the descendants of early town settlers and he had agreed to the listing.

The bronze model of the Mary and John is certainly an emblem of identity; a "collective representation" as well as a "condensation symbol." This is apparent from both the model and the metal plaques on the granite pedestal. The inscription on the front pedestal reads: "To the Men and Women Who Settled . . . from 1635 to 1650 and Founded Its Municipal, Social and Religious Life this Monument is Dedicated 1905." The plaque on the back of the pedestal is inscribed with a list of the first settlers' names. If, as Warner said of the Tercentenary, the images and ceremonies will not call up the souls of the ancestors, "they will at least evoke for the living the spirit that animated the generations that embodied the power and glory of yesterday" (Warner 1961:104).

The restoration and dedication of "higher rank emblems" such as the Mary and John model, I would suggest, do a bit more: they extend the collective identity they evoke beyond the lineal descendants of the early settlers to all those who through marriage, adoption of house lineages, residence, dramatic reenactment, anthropological, archaeological, and historical research, and in other ways seek to identify with the great tradition symbolized by the emblems. And the identity may continue indefinitely into the future if it is maintained by the descendants of the present generation of "oldtimers" and "newcomers" and adopted by future generations of "newcomers."

Whether in other forms, such as a model of the *Dreadnought* (Warner 1959:208), a colonial flag, or a sculptured eagle, emblems like the Mary and John model are signs with iconic, indexical, and symbolic features. Iconically they are replicas, or replicas of replicas of historical objects; indexically they denote or connote such objects through proper names and other indices. Symbolically, they address interpretants (and interpreters) in the form of a future self, descendants, and other persons addressed. The reference to the future is an essential component of the symbol, both because a self, a descendant, or other persons who interpret the emblem will continue or come into being in the future, and because the interpretations themselves are tentative and fallible, subject to correction by future genealogical, historical, and anthropological research. The authentic identity which the residents of "Yankee City," and perhaps all Americans, are looking for will not be found in the past. It can only emerge in the dialogue of interpretations about the emblems constructed in the past and in the present, and about those that will be constructed in the future. Many of the emblems will be the same, although many will change. Warner's concluding interpretation of the Tercentenary applies as well to the end of the 1970s if not to the Bicentennial years, and will probably continue to apply to the 1980s:

> Time in the aftermath of glory has run down; it is a period of diminution, of loss of meaning, when life is less vital, men less significant, and heroes harder to find. Symbolically, Yankee City has changed her image of herself. She has become another symbolic collectivity, with new collective representations to tell her what she is and express what she is to others. [Warner 1959:208.]

7

The development of a semiotics of emblems discussed in the preceding pages occurs in two distinct contexts: totemism among North American Indians and Australian aborigines, and the memorial rites and celebrations of a modern New England urban community. Durkheim (1915) was taken as a pioneer source for the former development and Warner (1959) as a pioneer source for the latter. That both developments involved a considerable interplay of ethnographic observation and speculative theory is obvious from the discussion. It may be useful to summarize, in this final section, some of the more problematic aspects of a semiotic theory of emblems in relation to the contexts in which it developed.

Durkheim's application of the analogy of totems with national flags and heraldic designs, brilliant and fruitful as it was, never transcended its context. That context included not only the ethnographic reports on North American and Australian totemism, but also an acquaintance with flags and heraldry he shared with his contemporaries.

There is no doubt that to have regarded a totem as a flag of the clan, carved and engraved in graphic designs upon everyday objects, having a sacred character related to the tribal religion and its cosmological and social systems of clasification, brought an exotic realm of unfamiliar practices and beliefs into the realm of the familiar and comprehensible.

Durkheim drew on current social psychological theories to speculate on why a soldier dies for his country's flag rather than for his country and on how assemblies of men need concrete, visual emblems to express and sustain their sentiments of social unity after the "effervescence" of their assemblies fades. He applied these theories to Australian totemism to argue that a totemic emblem as the symbol of the clan becomes the only permanent element of social life since there are no other sources of unity in a clan. "By definition it is common to all. . . . When generations change, it remains the same; it is the permanent element of social life" (1949:221).

Durkheim, however, was not always consistent in applying his symbolic theory of totemic emblems. When he appealed to the flag analogy to argue that the logic of modern science was born of the primitive logic of totemism, Durkheim interpreted the statement that man is a kangaroo as an identity statement, "like our saying that heat is a movement, or light is a vibration of the ether" (Durkheim 1947:238). In his analysis of emblems as badges or insignia of membership in a social group the statement "I am a Kangaroo" and the modern lodge member's "I am a Lion" would be almost exact parallels as identity statements. Both assert membership in a group whose totem, or mascot, is named in the statement, I would surmise.

An important implication of Durkheim's emblem theory is that the display of a graphic design of the totem can make a statement of identity (the emblem's "manifest identity") even in the absence of a verbal statement. Through such a statement of identity, between the graphic design and the object it represents, the displayer asserts membership in the group whose emblem is displayed (the emblem's "latent identity").

Levi-Strauss shares Durkheim's belief in the continuity between primitive and modern logic but disagrees with practically all the other features of Durkheim's theory. In fact, Levi-Strauss's critical review of totemism in 1963 echoes Goldenweiser's denial that totemism is a unitary and distinctive phenomenon, and leads him to the conclusion that "so-called totemism" or the "totemic illusion" is simply a miscellaneous collection of traits that are differently emphasized in different societies and cultures.

There is, however, a more positive side to Levi-Strauss's critique of totemism, as there also was to Goldenweiser's. For Levi-Strauss, "so-called totemism" is made intelligible in a structuralist framework but cannot be understood within the older functionalist, empirical, and naturalistic framework. Viewing totemism as a complex set of relations between systems of social units and systems of natural species, Levi-Strauss interprets it as a way of encoding the structural relations of social groups in the structural relations of natural species. The assumption that a similarity of structures exists between the two series, cultural and natural, is referred to by Levi-Strauss as "the postulate of homology."

While recent criticism has questioned the validity of characterizing Levi-Strauss's postulate as an empirical generalization, it cannot be denied that taken as an hypothesis, the postulate of homology has stimulated some fruitful discussion and research. It is also noteworthy that the structuralist interpretation of totemism is neither inconsistent with its being a unitary and distinctive phenomenon nor with functionalism. (Radcliffe-Brown demonstrated this double compatibility in his second paper on totemism, and Goldenweiser foreshadowed the convergence in his later papers.)

A problem that poses great difficulties for Levi-Strauss's approach is to explain how particular social groups, or their individual members, come to be identified by some particular emblem or totem. This problem was already recognized by Radcliffe-Brown and he clearly stated the need of a general theory. The problem is more acute for Levi-Strauss because he not only rejects Durkheim's theory of "effervescence" and sentiments as causes, but also rejects Radcliffe-Brown's natural interest theory, according to which particular species are chosen as totems because they have already become objects of ritual attitudes for some practical reasons. Levi-Strauss insists that these species are chosen because they are "good to think" and not because they are "good to eat" and squarely confronts the challenge of showing how his postulate of homologous structures can account for the association of particular members of the natural series (species of plants and animal species) with particular members of the cultural series (clans and other social groups). He displays impressive ingenuity on a wide range of ethnographic information to deal with this problem in his book on *The Savage Mind*. He even introduces a concept of "homological particularization" to derive a structural homology between the members of social groups and the members of species, from the structural homology between the social groups and the species. He suggests, à la Radcliffe-Brown, that the categorical schemes of classification based on structural oppositions can, and do, absorb all sorts of social oppositions as well. In consequence, a society with a totemic cosmology "does not confine itself to abstract contemplation of a system of correspondence but rather furnishes the individual members of these segments with a pretext and sometimes even a provocation to distinguish themselves by their behavior" (Levi-Strauss 1966:169, 170).

In spite of his lucid presentation of the problem and his promising outline of its solution, Levi-Strauss's detailed analysis is somewhat disappointing. He formulates the technical question in terms of whether proper names have any "meaning" or "signification" and argues that "the ultimate diversity of individual and collective beings" can be represented by systems of proper names that "always signify membership of an actual or virtual class, which must be either that of the person named or the person giving the name" (ibid., p. 185).

Levi-Strauss's reduction of proper names to classes implies that totemic names are names of abstract concepts and not names of concrete individuals or collections of individuals. (This implication is also drawn by Stanner on the basis of his ethnographic acquaintance with Australian aborigines.) His conclusion that primitives never name, that they always classify, was probably motivated by a desire to do justice to the capacities of the "savage mind." The conclusion is misguided, however laudable its motivation. At issue is not whether Australians classify or construct iconic images; that they do so has been recognized for a long time. Rather, the question is how particular totems and totemic emblems come to denote particular individuals or social groups. This question is not likely to be satisfactorily answered by reducing individuals to classes and the relations of individuals to structural homologies between the relations of classes and between the relations of relations.

I have argued that under the influence of Radcliffe-Brown's functional structuralism, Durkheim's emblem theory was eclipsed and the identity problem remained unsolved until the emblem theory was revived and significantly extended by Warner in his Murngin (1937) and Yankee City (1959) monographs. Warner integrated Durkheim's theory with a general analysis of symbols and symbol systems and with impressive empirical detail he showed how particular emblems, in sacred as well as in secular ritual contexts, came historically to be identified with particular social groups and individuals.

Although Warner's symbolic analysis of emblems appears quite eclectic,[6] it has a cohesiveness worthy of Peirce's general theory of signs or semiotic. While Peirce did not construct a semiotics of emblems, I have tried to show that much of his general theory of signs is relevant for a semiotics of emblems. Precisely, it is the manner in which Peirce's theory of signs enables us to show how the structural (or iconic) and the denotative (or indexical) features of signs and sign systems combine with one another and with verbal components that

[6] Warner acknowledged that his general theory of symbols was derived from Ogden and Richards, Freud, Jung, Pareto, Piaget, G.H. Mead, Sapir, and Charles Morris, among others. That the last three contributors were all at the University of Chicago just before or during the periods that Radcliffe-Brown and Warner taught there is a significant coincidence from the point of view of the development of a pragmatic, social, and semiotic anthropology.

makes the theory applicable to a semiotics of emblems and the identity problem. (For a recent application to an Australian naming system see Silverstein 1981.)

Warner's reversal of Durkheim's analogy, "the totem is the flag of the clan" to "the flag is the totem of Yankee City," was not only a cultural shock tactic applied to the study of a modern American community; it was also a genuine, pioneering effort to discover the collective and individual representations that form the enduring and permanent center of social life and evoke in a society's members the unifying sentiments of loyalty and identity.

In his Australian study Warner found such collective symbols of identity in the higher-rank totemic emblems and the local waterholes where the ancestral spirits are invoked. Correspondingly, in his Yankee City study he thought he found a collective symbol of "ultimate identification and belongingness" in the society of The Sons and Daughters of the First Settlers: "It said—and they and the community said—that they completely belonged, and they were so identified." But since only a small fraction of Yankee City's residents can trace their ancestry over 300 years to the first settlers, this symbol of identity is not common to all residents. (In fairness to Warner, he did not interpret it as a symbol of the melting pot or of the American Dream; rather, he regarded it as a standard of the ideal "Yankee" American identity by which to measure the hierarchical scale of "ethnic" approximations in a "time-table for assimilation.")

In updating Warner's Yankee City study, I have found that the emblems of an American identity are probably closer to a melting pot ideal now than they were at the time of Warner's original study. Paradoxically, the contemporary situation is also a closer parallel to the Australian model than was the case in the 1930s.

As my paper argues, two trends of change have preserved emblems of Yankee City's past while bringing new groups and individuals under the emblems' latent identities. One trend concerns the way in which "ethnics" and "newcomers" have "matured" into "Yankees" and "oldtimers" after at least two generations of local birth and residence in addition to the adoption of a life style acceptable to the community. The second trend is represented by the way in which the society of

The Sons and Daughters has been expanding its membership and guest lists to include people who are not lineal descendants of first settlers. The emblems, iconic and verbal, have in both cases preserved more or less the same manifest identities while their latent identities have expanded.

The situation in Yankee City might be comparable to the aboriginal Australian one, as Yengoyan, in fact, has recently suggested to me. There, too, the importance of a two-generation genealogy, a group-conforming life style, and myths of origin from the local waterhole are associated with totemic emblems and their cults. Another and equally appropriate interpretation of Yankee City's emblems of identity is, as I have suggested, in terms of a Peircean semiotic as illustrated by the unveiling of the bronze model of the Mary and John.

Clearly, a semiotics of emblems is not the only possible method for interpreting emblems. Nor is it a method of studying symbols in anthropology that replaces functionalist, structuralist, and other possible approaches. However, a semiotic anthropology does include both functionalism and structuralism, and furthermore is capable of embracing a fruitful competition of variant models, as the work of Geertz and Schneider, V. Turner and T. Turner, Friedrich, Silverstein, and Sahlins now attests.

ACKNOWLEDGEMENTS

Approximately half of this paper was read as one of the 1980 Harry Hoijer Lectures on Symbols in Anthropology at the University of California, Los Angeles. I am grateful to the UCLA Department of Anthropology, and especially to Professor Jacques Maquet, Chairman of the Department, for the opportunity to join them in honoring Professor Hoijer's distinguished career and his contributions to anthropology.

The research on which this paper is based was made possible by a small grant from the National Institute of Mental Health in the summer of 1977 for the collection of data on the changing character of ethnicity in an urban community, and by a Rockefeller Foundation Humanities Fellowship in 1978–79 for the study of diversity and unity in a changing American identity. I am also grateful to Douglas Goodfriend and Elizabeth Jacoby for their valuable help in this field, and to Erika Reiner. My wife's wide-ranging knowledge, her sensitive perceptions of people and places, and her uncanny eye for crucial archival finds have been indispensable for my research and writing. I am grateful to Nancy Cutler Daniels for copyediting the manuscript and for helping me at the last moment to shorten it by 5000 words. I wish to thank Max Fisch, Paul Friedrich, Michael Silverstein, and Aram Yengoyan who gave me the benefit of their respective specialized knowledge in carefully reading the paper and suggesting several useful changes.

REFERENCES

1959   *The American College Dictionary,* ed. by C. Barnhart. New York: Random House.

1976   *The Concise Oxford Dictionary of Current English,* sixth edition, ed. by J.B. Sykes. London: Oxford University Press.

Boon, J.A.
1979   Saussure/Peirce a propos Language, Society and Culture. *Semiotica* 27: 83–101.

Boon, J.A. and D.M. Schneider
1974   Kinship vis-a-vis Myth: Contrasts in Levi-Strauss' Approaches to Cross-Cultural Comparison. *American Anthropologist* 76: 799–817.

Buchler, J., ed.
1955   *Philosophical Writings of Peirce.* New York: Dover Publications. [Original ed., 1940.]

Crane, W.
1912   Art and Character. In *Character and Life, A Symposium,* ed. by P.L. Parker. London: Williams and Norgate.

1914   *The Bases of Design.* London: G. Bell and Sons. [Original ed., 1898.]

Curley, J.M.
   1931   *Tercentenary of the Founding of Boston*. Boston City Coun-
          cil.

Dumont, L.
   1970   *Homo Hierarchicus*. Trans. by M. Sainsbury. Chicago:
          University of Chicago Press.

Durkheim, E.
   1947   *The Elementary Forms of the Religious Life*. Glencoe: The
          Free Press. [Original ed., 1915.]

Eco, J.
   1976   *A Theory of Semiotics*. Bloomington: Indiana University
          Press.

Firth, R.
   1973   *Symbols: Public and Private*. Ithaca: Cornell University
          Press.

Fortes, M.
   1966   Totem and Taboo. In *Proceedings of the Royal Anthro-
          pological Institute of Great Britain and Ireland*. London:
          Richard Madley Ltd., pp. 5–22.

Freud, S.
   1938   The Interpretation of Dreams. In *The Basic Writings of
          Sigmund Freud*. Trans. and ed. by A.A. Brill. New York:
          The Modern Library, pp. 35–150. [Original ed. 1900.]

Friedrich, P.
   1978   *The Meaning of Aphrodite*. Chicago: University of Chicago
          Press.

Geertz, C.
   1973   Religion as a Cultural System. In *The Interpretation of
          Cultures*. New York: Basic Books, pp. 87–126. [Original,
          1966.]

          Art as a Cultural System. Modern Language Notes 91:
          1473–99.

   1980   Blurred Genres: The Refiguration of Social Thought. *The
          American Scholar* 49: 165–79.

Gilman, E.B.
  1980   Word and Image in Quarles' 'Emblemes.' *Critical Inquiry* 6: 385–410.

Goldenweiser, A.
  1910   Totemism: An Analytical Study. *Journal of American Folklore* 23: 179–293.

  1918   Form and Content in Totemism. *American Anthropologist* 20: 280–95.

  1931   Totemism: An Essay on Religion and Society. In *The Making of Man,* ed. by V.F. Calverton. New York: Modern Library. Reprinted in abridged form in *Reader in Comparative Religion,* ed. by W.A. Lessa and E.Z. Vogt, New York: Harper and Row, 1965, pp. 363–92.

  1937   *Anthropology, An Introduction to Primitive Culture.* New York: F.S. Crofts & Co.

Hiatt, L.R.
  1969   Totemism Tomorrow: The Future of an Illusion. *Mankind* 7: 83–93.

Jakobson, R.
  1971   Visual and Auditory Signs. In *Selected Writings II*. The Hague: Mouton.

Kipling, R.
  1940   *Rudyard Kipling's Verse*. Definitive Edition. Garden City, N.Y.: Doubleday.

Leach, E.R.
  1961   Rethinking Anthropology. In *Rethinking Anthropology*. London: University of London, The Athlone Press, pp. 1–28.

Levi-Strauss, C.
  1963   *Totemism*. Boston: Beacon Press. [Original ed. in French, 1962.]

  1963a The Bear and the Barber. *The Journal of the Royal Anthropological Institute* XCIII: 1–11.

1966   *The Savage Mind*. London: Weidenfeld and Nicholson. [Original ed. in French, 1962.]

1976   *Structural Anthropology,* Vol. III. New York: Basic Books.

Linton, R.
1924   Totemism and the A.E.F. *American Anthropologist* 26: 296–300. Reprinted in *Reader in Comparative Religion,* ed. by W.A. Lessa and E.Z. Vogt, New York: Harper and Row, 1965.

Lyons, J.
1977   *Semantics*. 2 vols. Cambridge: Cambridge University Press.

Marquand, J.P.
1960   *Timothy Dexter Revisited*. Boston: Little, Brown and Co.

Munn, N.D.
1973   *Walbiri Iconography*. Ithaca: Cornell University Press.

Musee Guimet
1964   *Emblemes Totems Blasons*. Paris: Ministere D'Etat Affaires Culturelles.

Nadel, S.F.
1964   *The Foundations of Social Anthropology*. Glencoe: The Free Press. [Original ed., 1951.]

Ong, W.J.
1959   From Allegory to the Diagram in the Renaissance Mind. *Journal of Esthetics and Art Criticism* XVII.

Oppenheim, A.L.
1964   *Ancient Mesopotamia, Portrait of a Dead Civilization*. Chicago: University of Chicago Press.

Peirce, C.S.
1931–   *Collected Papers*. Vols. 1–6, ed. by C. Hartshorne and
1958   P. Weiss. Vols. 7–8, ed. by A.W. Burks. Cambridge: Harvard University Press.

Praz, M.
1964 *Studies in Seventeenth Century Imagery.* Second edition. Roma: Edizioni di Storia e Letteratura. [Original ed., 1939.]

Radcliffe-Brown, A.R.
1952 The Sociological Theory of Totemism. In *Structure and Function in Primitive Society.* London: Cohen and West, Ltd. [Original, 1929.]

1958 The Comparative Method in Social Anthropology. In *Method in Social Anthropology,* ed. by M.N. Srinivas. Chicago: University of Chicago Press, pp. 108–29. [Original, 1952.]

Redfield, R.
1962 Art and Icon. In *Human Nature and the Study of Society: The Papers of Robert Redfield,* ed. by M.P. Redfield. Chicago: University of Chicago Press, pp. 468–89.

Sahlins, M.
1976 *Culture and Practical Reason.* Chicago: University of Chicago Press.

Sapir, E.
1927 Anthropology and Sociology. In *The Social Sciences and Their Interrelations,* ed. by W.F. Ogburn and A. Goldenweiser. Boston: Houghton Mifflin. Reprinted in Sapir, 1949.

1949 Symbolism. In *Selected Writings of Edward Sapir in Language, Culture and Personality,* ed. by D.G. Mandelbaum. Berkeley: University of California Press, pp. 564–68. [Original, 1934.]

Schneider, D.M.
1969 Kinship, Nationality and Religion in American Culture: Towards a Definition of Kinship. In *Forms of Symbolic Action,* ed. by R.F. Spencer. Proceedings of the American Ethnological Society. Seattle: University of Washington Press, pp. 116–25.

1979   Kinship, Community and Locality in American Culture. In *Kin and Communities*, ed. by A.J. Lichtman and J.R. Challinor. Washington, D.C.: The Smithsonian Institute, pp. 155–74.

Schoolcraft, H.

1851   *Historical and Statistical Information Respecting the History, Condition and Prospect of the Indian Tribes of the United States*. Philadelphia: Lippincott and Co.

Schwartz, T.

1975   Cultural Totemism: Ethnic Identity, Primitive and Modern. In *Ethnic Identity, Cultural Continuities and Change*, ed. by G. DeVos and L. Romanucii-Ross. Palo Alto: Mayfield Publishing Co.

Sebeok, T.A.

1975   Six Species of Signs: Some Propositions and Strictures. *Semiotica* 13: 233–60.

Silverstein, M.

1976   Shifters, Linguistic Categories and Cultural Description. In *Meaning in Anthropology*, ed. by K. Baso and H. Selby. Albuquerque: University of New Mexico Press.

1981   Naming Sets Among the Worora. In *Proceedings of the American Ethnological Society*, ed. by H. Conklin.

Singer, M.

1973   *A Neglected Source of Structuralism: Radcliffe-Brown, Whitehead and Russell*. A.S.A. Colloquium, Oxford University, England. (In absentia)

1977   On the Symbolic and Historic Structure of an American Identity. *Ethos* 5: 428–54.

1978   For a Semiotic Anthropology. In *Sight, Sound and Sense*, ed. by T.A. Sebeok. Bloomington: Indiana University Press.

1980   *When a Great Tradition Modernizes*. Chicago: University of Chicago Press. [Original ed., 1972.]

1980 Signs of the Self: An Exploration in Semiotic Anthropology. *American Anthropologist* 82: 485–507.

1981 Personal and Social Identity in Dialogue. In *New Approaches to the Self,* ed. by B. Lee. New York: Plenum.

Stanner, W.E.H.
1965 Religion, Totemism and Symbolism. In *Aboriginal Man in Australia,* ed. by R.M. and C.G. Berndt. Sydney: Angus and Robertson.

Tarn, N.
1976 The Heraldic Vision: A Cognitive Model for Comparative Aesthetics. *Alcheringa: Ethnopoetics* Vol. 2, n.z.

Thernstrom, S.
1971 *Poverty and Progress: Social Mobility in a Nineteenth Century City.* New York: Atheneum. [Orig. ed., 1964.]

Turner, T.
1980 The Social Skin. In *Not Work Alone: A Cross-Cultural View of Activities Superfluous to Survival,* ed. by J. Cherfas and R. Lewin. London: Temple Smith.

Turner, V.
1967 Symbols in Ndembu Ritual. In *The Forest of Symbols.* Ithaca: Cornell University Press, pp. 19–47. [Orig. paper pub. in 1964.]

Umiker-Sebeok, E.J. and T.A. Sebeok, eds.
1976 *Aboriginal Sign Languages of the Americas and Australia.* New York: Plenum Press.

Uspensky, B.
1976 *The Semiotics of the Russian Icon,* ed. by S. Ruby. Lisse: DeRidder Press.

Veblen, T.
1899 *The Theory of the Leisure Class.* New York: MacMillan. Reprinted New York: Kelley, 1965.

Waddington, C.H.
    1974   Horse Brands of the Mongolians: A System of Signs in a Nomadic Culture. *American Ethnologist 1: 471–88.*

Wagner, A.
    1978   *Heralds and Ancestors.* London: The British Museum.

Wallis, M.
    1975   *Art and Signs.* Bloomington: Indiana University Press.

Warner, W.L.
    1959   *The Living and the Dead: A Study of the Symbolic Life of Americans.* New Haven: Yale University Press.

    1961   *The Family of God: A Symbolic Study of Christian Life in America.* New Haven: Yale University Press.

    1963   *Yankee City.* New Haven: Yale University Press.

    1964   *A Black Civilization: A Study of an Australian Tribe.* New York: Harper Torchbook. [Original ed., 1937.]

Warner, W.L. and P.S. Lunt
    1941   *The Social Life of a Modern Community.* New Haven: Yale University Press.

Warner, W.L. and L. Srole
    1945   *The Social Systems of American Ethnic Groups.* New Haven: Yale University Press.

White, T.H.
    1978   *In Search of History: A Personal Adventure.* New York: Harper and Row.

Wolf, E.
    1958   The Virgin of Guadalupe: A Mexican National Symbol. *Journal of American Folklore LXXI: 34–9.*

Yengoyan, A.A.
    1979   Economy, Society and Myth in Aboriginal Australia. In *Annual Review of Anthropology* 8: 393–415.

Zimmer, H.
    1962   *Myth and Symbols in Indian Art and Civilization.* New York: Harper and Brothers. [Original ed., 1946.]

OUR CONTRIBUTORS

JAMES W. FERNANDEZ is professor and chairman, Department of Anthropology, Princeton University. He received his Ph.D. from Northwestern University in 1962. He has conducted field research in Gabon, South Africa, Zambia, Ghana, Togo, Dahomey, and Spain. Among his research interests are the dynamics of culture change and acculturation, symbolic interaction and integration, expressive culture, religious movements, and metaphoric and metonymic extensions. His publications include "The Mission of the Metaphor in Expressive Culture" (1974), *Fang Architectonics* (1977), "The Performance of Ritual Metaphors" (1977), and "Symbolic Anthropology Evolving" (1977).

MILTON SINGER is professor emeritus, Department of Anthropology, and Paul Klapper Professor of the Social Sciences, University of Chicago. He received his Ph.D. from Chicago in 1940. He has conducted field research in India and New England. His research interests include innovation and tradition in India and the U.S., semiotic anthropology, and philosophic anthropology. Among his publications are *When a Great Tradition Modernizes: An Anthropological Approach to Indian Civilization* (1972), "Robert Redfield's Development of a Social Anthropology of Civilizations" (1974), "On the Symbolic and Historic Structure of an American Identity" (1977), "For a Semiotic Anthropology" (1978), and "Signs of the Self" (1980).

MELFORD E. SPIRO is professor of Anthropology, University of California, San Diego. He received his Ph.D. from Northwestern University in 1950. He has conducted field research in Wisconsin (Ojibwa Indians), Micronesia, Israel, Burma, and Thailand. His research interests include psychological anthropology, the dynamics of culture and personality, and comparative religion. Among his publications are *Kibbutz: Venture in Utopia* (1956), *Children of the Kibbutz* (1958), *Burmese Supernaturalism* (1967), *Buddhism and Society* (1971), *Kinship and Marriage in Burma* (1977), and *Gender and Culture: Kibbutz Women Revisited* (1979).

THE EDITOR

JACQUES MAQUET is professor and chairman, Department of Anthropology, UCLA. He received his Ph.D. (social anthropology) from the University of London in 1952; in addition he holds a LL.D. and D.Phil. from the University of Louvain, as well as a D.Lit. from the University of Paris. He has conducted field research in Rwanda, Uganda, Zaire, and Sri Lanka. His research interests include the sociology of knowledge, analysis of societal networks, and the development of an anthropological perspective in aesthetic phenomena, symbolic systems, and "socially constructed realities." Among his publications are *The Sociology of Knowledge* (1951), *The Premise of Inequality in Ruanda* (1961), *Power and Society in Africa* (1971), *Civilizations of Black Africa* (1972), *Africanity* (1972), and *Introduction to Aesthetic Anthropology* (1979).